FREE FROM ALL ERROR

FREE FROM ALL ERROR

AUTHORSHIP, INERRANCY,
HISTORICITY OF SCRIPTURE,
CHURCH TEACHING AND
MODERN SCRIPTURE SCHOLARS

by
Fr. William G. Most

Marytown Press
1600 West Park Avenue
Libertyville, Illinois 60048
847-367-7800

©1985, 1990 (revised), 2009 Marytown Press
All rights reserved.

ISBN: 0-913382-51-5

Marytown Press
1600 West Park Avenue, Libertyville, Illinois 60048. 847-367-7800

CONTENTS

ACKNOWLEDGMENTS

Biblical quotations are from the Revised Standard Version of the Bible, Catholic Edition (1965, 1966).

Raymond E. Brown, "The Myth of the Gospels Without Myth," *St. Anthony Messenger* (May 1971), pp. 44-46.

Raymond E. Brown, *The Birth of the Messiah* (Garden City, New York: Doubleday & Co., 1977).

Raymond E. Brown, *The Critical Meaning of the Bible* (New York: Paulist Press, 1981).

Thomas A. Hoffman, "Inspiration, Normativeness, Canonicity and the Unique Sacred Character of the Bible," *Catholic Biblical Quarterly* (July 1982), pp. 447-46

R. Lewin, "Evolutionary Theory Under Fire," *Science News,* Vol. 210 (November 21, 1980), pp. 883-887.

A. J. Mattill, "The Value of Acts as a Source for the Study of Paul," *Perspectives on Luke-Acts,* Charles H. Talbert, ed. Special Studies Series No. 5 (Danville, Virginia: [National] Association of Baptist Professors of Religion, 1978), pp. 76-98.

Norman Perrin, *Rediscovering the Teaching of Jesus* (New York: Harper & Row, 1967).

DOCUMENTS

Leo XIII Encyclical *Providentissimus Deus*, November 18, 1893. Apostolic Letter *Vigilantiae*, October 30, 1902.

St. Pius X Apostolic Letter *Quoniam in re biblica*, March 27, 1906. *Motu Proprio, Praestantia Sacrae Scripturae*, November 18, 1907.

Benedict XV Encyclical *Spiritus Paraclitus*, September 15, 1920.

Pius XII Encyclical *Divino Afflante Spiritu*, September 30, 1943. Apostolic Letter *In cotidianis precibus*, March 24, 1945. Encyclical *Humani Generis*, August 12, 1950.

The Pontifical Biblical Commission Responses 1905-1933. Letter to Bishops of Italy, August 20, 1941. On Vernacular Versions, August 22, 1943. Letter to Cardinal Suhard, January 16, 1948. Instruction, May 13, 1950. Instruction, December 15, 1955. *Monitum*, June 20, 1961. Instruction on the Historical Truth of the Gospels (On Form Criticism), April 21, 1964.

John XXIII Address to The Pontifical Biblical Institute, February 17, 1960.

Holy Office *Monitum*, June 20, 1961.

Vatican II *Constitution on Divine Revelation*, November 18, 1965.

Note: Most of these documents can be had in Latin in *Enchiridion Biblicum*. An English edition of most of them is, *Rome and the Study of Scripture*, St. Meinrad's, 1964. Numbering in some places differs from that in the *Enchiridion Biblicum*. But *Rome and the Study of Scripture* includes excerpts from an article by Athanasius Miller, a secretary of The Biblical Commission, which was not approved by the Commission. Rather Msgr. John Steinmueller, a consultor of the Commission at that time declares in his book, *The Sword of the Spirit* (Stella Maris Books, 1977, p. 78, note) that Miller and another secretary, who had published a similar statement, were almost brought before the Holy Office for making such statements.

Chapter 1

Inspiration and Authorship

The most remarkable fact concerning Holy Scripture is that it is not only the Word of God but that God Himself, the Holy Spirit, is its chief author. This the Church tells us. At the same time, the Church also says that there is a human author, who remains free yet infallibly does what God wants him to do. How is all of this possible? What does it really mean to say that God is the author?

Before answering those questions, another important fact strikes us. A record from the fifth or sixth century of the Church states for the first time that God is the author of Holy Scripture. *Ancient Statutes of the Church,* a document from that period, says that a man who is to be ordained a bishop must first be asked "if he believes that God is the one and same author of the New and Old Testament. . . ."

There are earlier statements about Scripture, but there is none in which God is explicitly identified as their author. For example, about 95 A.D. Pope St. Clement I wrote this to Corinth: "You have studied the sacred writings, which are true, which are through the Holy Spirit" (1:45).

Athenagoras, a second century apologist, spoke of the Holy Spirit as using the human writers "as if a flutist breathed into his flute" (*Legation* 9). A bit later, about 181 A.D., St Theophilus of Antioch wrote, "Moses . . . or rather, the Word of God, who used him as an instrument, said, 'In the beginning God made heaven and earth'" (*To Autolycus* 2:10). Around 200 A.D. St. Hippolytus said of the prophets that "like instruments, always having the Word of God as a plectrum (a pick), united with themselves, in themselves, when moved by Him, they announced what God willed" (*On Antichrist* 2).

While not explicitly saying that God is the author of Holy Scripture, these texts present the concept of God's authorship because He uses humans as instruments.

It will be both interesting and helpful to investigate how it is that only after five or six centuries of existence did the Church clearly teach that God is the author of Holy Scripture. The key is found in the words of our Lord at the Last Supper: "The Holy Spirit . . . will teach you all things, and bring to your remembrance all I have said to you" (John 14:26). This text does not mean that there would be new revelations. No, the great Deposit of Faith was complete when the last Apostle died and the New Testament was finished. After that point, we receive no new public revelation, though there are private revelations. (The word *private* is not very helpful, but it is standard; even Fatima, though addressed to the world, is technically a private revelation.)

Our Lord promised the Church, not new revelations, but an ever deeper penetration into the Deposit of Faith. A striking instance is the teaching on the Immaculate Conception, which was defined by Pope Pius IX in 1854. Was the dogma of the Immaculate Conception so clearly present in Scripture so that without the help of the Church one could see it? Not really. But with the help of the Church, we know, thanks to Pius IX, that this dogma is implied in the words of God to the serpent in Genesis 3:15: "I will put enmity between you and the woman, and between your seed and her seed." The dogma of the Immaculate Conception is similarly implied in the greeting of the archangel to the Virgin Mary: "Hail full of grace" (Luke 1:28). (It should be noted that there is debate about the interpretation of Genesis 3:15 and the translation of Luke 1:28.)

So, if Mary was never under the dominion of Satan, being in a perpetual state of enmity with him, she must have been immaculately conceived. Similarly, her being "full of grace" implies the grace of the Immaculate Conception. Nonetheless we need the help of the Church to be sure of these implications.

What of the words of the Fathers of the first centuries? Teachings found in the early Fathers are thought to imply the Immaculate Conception. They often spoke in glowing, sweeping terms about Mary's holiness. That could imply an Immaculate Conception. Again, the Fathers, practically all of them, speak of Mary as a New Eve.

2

St. Paul had called our Lord "a New Adam"—the new head of the race, who reverses the damage resulting from the sin of the first Adam. The Fathers add that Mary shares in that work, in undoing the harm resulting from the sin of the first Eve. But then, one could argue: If Mary is the New Eve, and since the first Eve had no sin when she began her existence, Mary must have been conceived immaculate. The trouble here is that not one of the Fathers ever reasoned in this way about the Immaculate Conception.

Since both Scripture and the Fathers were unclear regarding Mary's immaculateness, there was room for denial. And denial came from a surprising source: St. Bernard of Clairvaux. In the twelfth century, Bernard, who was so fond of devotion to Mary, clearly denied Mary's Immaculate Conception. Beginning with St. Bernard, then, most of the major theologians of the Middle Ages, including even St. Thomas Aquinas, denied the Immaculate Conception.

The tide began to turn with the help of Duns Scotus (c. 1265-1308). Gradually the popes began siding with the arguments for the doctrine of the Immaculate Conception. The result was that a century and a half before the definition of the Immaculate Conception, the whole Church had come to believe the doctrine.

Now we can see that the Immaculate Conception was quite unclear, even dim, in the first centuries of the Church. Yet later, under the promised guidance of the Holy Spirit, the Church was enabled to see it clearly, even to define it. Therefore, we need not be surprised to find, at a comparatively late date, a statement by the Church that God is the principal author of Holy Scripture.

Additional statements by the Church were to follow, after some centuries. For example, Peter, Bishop of Antioch, asked Pope Leo IX to send him a correct profession of faith. Leo complied. "I believe," wrote the Pope, " . . . that there is one author of the New and Old Testament, of the law and Prophets and Apostles, God, and almighty Lord" (April 13, 1053). We find many similar statements later: in the Council of Florence (1441); in the Council of Trent (1546); in Leo XIII's *Providentissimus Deus* (1893); in Benedict XV's *Spiritus Paraclitus* (1920); in Pius XII's *Divino Afflante Spiritu* (1943).

Vatican II, in its *Constitution on Divine Revelation*, n.11, taught that "Holy Mother Church, from the apostolic faith, considers the entire books of the Old and New Testament, with all their parts, as sacred and canonical because, being written under the inspiration of the Holy Spirit, they have God as their author. . . ."

Having accepted the Church's pronouncement, we still need to know what it means to say that God is the chief author of Scripture. In other words, precisely how does He interact with the human writer?

A few authors suggest that God dictated the words of Scripture to the human writer, as a man might dictate to a secretary. But then the question arises as to how the human being could also be called an author? And what of the words of St. Paul in 1 Corinthians 1:14-18, where Paul's memory wakes up, as it were, in stages?

First Paul says he is glad that he baptized only two persons, Crispus and Gaius, so those clique-loving Corinthians could not say that they had such a special attachment to St. Paul. Then he adds, as his memory awakens, that he also baptized the household of Stephanas. And, in a further awakening, he adds that he is not sure if he baptized any others. Such a gradual gathering of recollections hardly coincides with the idea that the omniscient God was dictating those words to Paul. Though the Church has never condemned it, this theory of dictation was generally given up by the end of the nineteenth century.

In the sixteenth century, Sixtus of Siena suggested that Scripture was a merely human product that the Church later approved. In this view, of course, God would not be the author of Scripture at all. Hence Vatican Council I explicitly rejected this theory, saying, "The Church however considers them [the books of Scripture] sacred and canonical, not because they were written by mere human industry and were then approved by her authority, nor because they contain revelation without error, but because, since they were written by the inspiration of the Holy Spirit, they have God as their author" (*Enchiridion Biblicum*, Arnodo, Romae, 1954, p. 77).

Vatican I also said that it would not be enough to say that the books of Scripture "contain revelation without error." They do that, of course, but that point alone would not be enough to establish the fact that God is actually the author of Scripture. To contain revelation without error is largely negative. It is a protection against mistakes, which is different from divine authorship.

Late in the nineteenth century, Cardinal Franzelin developed a different theory of inspiration, which enjoyed much popularity for a while. He thought that divine inspiration affected the human writer only as far as the content of Scripture was concerned. The composition and verbal expression, Franzelin thought, were contributed by the human writer.

This theory was an improvement over the earlier attempts, but it, too, was insufficient. It made an artificial division, and did not adequately explain how God can really be called the author. The view of Cardinal Franzelin, accordingly, has been abandoned.

M. J. Lagrange, a great Scripture scholar closer to our time, suggested that inspiration is primarily a divine illumination of the mind of the human writer, making him able to judge in a higher, clearer, and more certain light. But again, this seems more like assistance on the part of God, not authorship by God.

Pierre Benoit, in 1965, suggested that God's influence on the speculative mind of the human writer was a revelation. That is, it gave the writer new content, new material, while God's influence on the practical working of the man's mind, in composition and communication, would be called inspiration. But inspiration does not always or necessarily include revelation of facts not previously known to the human author.

Drawing on some of the more recent statements of the Church, let us attempt to go beyond these theories. Pope Pius XII, in his great Encyclical *Divino Afflante Spiritu* (1943), wrote this: "The sacred writer in producing the sacred book is the organon, that is, the instrument of the Holy Spirit, an instrument living and endowed with reason.   .   . He, working under inspiration, still uses his own faculties and powers in such a way that all can easily gather from the book he produces 'the proper character, and, as it were, the individual lines and characteristics' of the human writer."

Pius XII was quoting, in part, from the *Spiritus Paraclitus* of Pope Benedict XV (1920). He wanted to draw the lines in such a way that both God and the human writer would be true authors, even though God would be the principal author, really in control of the situation. To bring out the role of God, the Pope spoke of God as the principal cause, the human as the instrumental cause. Yet, to show that the human was not like a lifeless instrument—a pen or a typewriter—he added that the human writer did utilize his own talents and powers so that his distinctive style and character became apparent. Hence we see how it is that not all things in Scripture are in magnificent literary style. If God alone had produced them, of course, they would be. But the human writer retains his own characteristics, even under inspiration.

How is such a combination as this possible? God is transcendent, completely above and beyond our categories and classifications. His knowing is unlike ours. Human beings have both an active and a passive way of knowing things. When we know in a passive way, we take on an impression from outside ourselves, much as a tablet of wax takes on the impression of a signet ring. But this cannot be the way in which God knows. He would then be receiving something He did not have before. He cannot receive for He lacks nothing. When a human knows actively, he knows something is happening simply because he is causing it. A blind man pushing a chair knows the chair is moving because he is pushing it. But while the blind man is limited, God is not. The active way is not a complete explanation, but it is a small part of the answer.

Therefore, God's way of knowing is unlike any knowing we can imagine. It is simply transcendent. Similarly, God can use a human as an instrument, insuring that the human writes all God wants, as He wants, yet leaving the human writer free to utilize his own human skills and characteristics.

A comparison may be helpful. We want to consider two modes, or manners, in which God affects people by his grace, even outside of inspiration. First, through ordinary actual graces, God guides and moves a person to reach the right thought and decision in a process that is commonly done step-by-step. This is a discursive process. In this mode, God works mostly through the human faculties, causing them, as it were, to churn out the needed effect in such a way that the human being is active too, while receiving all the power to act from God.

But there is a higher manner in which God moves souls. It is by way of the Gifts of the Holy Spirit. (The Gifts are not confined to moving a man to decide and act; they do other things too. But here we are considering only one kind of effect of the Gifts.) When God moves a man via the Gifts, the man does not need any step-by-step process to reach the right idea and decision. The answer is, as it were, dropped ready-made into the hopper of his mind. The man's human faculties have little to do with generating the thought. The man's cooperation consists largely in consenting to be moved in this way.

Something comparable happens when God inspires a human writer. The human writer's faculties and powers are indeed somewhat active (not as active as in the first mode), and somewhat passive (as in the case of a man being moved by the Gifts). In this way, God has full control, fully produces the sacred book; yet the human puts his imprint on the style and expression as much as even a lifeless instrument would do when handled by an artist.

So we can see how two things can be said in the book of the prophet Amos. In chapter one, we see that we are about to read "the words of Amos." Yet at the end of the same short book, we find: "Says the Lord your God."

Chapter 2

Which Books Are Inspired?

We saw in chapter 1 that Holy Scripture has God for its author. But how do we know just which books are inspired and have God as author? If someone were to reply that we just accept the decision of the Church, the answer would not be incorrect. But there would still seem to be a danger of reasoning in a vicious circle, in which we say that we believe that these books are inspired because the Church tells us they are inspired and that we believe the Church because inspired Scripture shows that Christ gave the Church the mandate to teach.

There is a way out of this circle. To find it, it will help if we review some attempts that simply do not work.

Long ago, in 1910, Professor Gerald Birney Smith, of the University of Chicago, gave a paper to the 28th annual Baptist Congress. The next year it was published, somewhat revised, in *The Biblical World* 37 (pp. 19-29). Smith's frankness was really remarkable. He reviewed every way he knew to determine which books are or are not inspired. (In the first centuries, many works were circulating as Gospels, with the names of various apostles on them, yet those books are not accepted as inspired today. Hence our question.)

Professor Smith said: "The exact determination of the Canon of Scripture [list of inspired books] was never a burning issue until after the Reformation. . . . It was only when Luther denied the authority of the Church and appealed to the Word of God alone that there was felt to be any pressing need for defining the exact list of authoritative books." Before Luther, of course, people accepted the teaching of the Catholic

Church. But once he and his associates rejected the Church's authority and tried to appeal to Scripture alone, it became necessary to ask which books are inspired.

Professor Smith then explains how Luther worked. "Luther proposed a practical test. . . . The distinction which he actually had in mind was between those writings which have the power to bring to men the assurance of forgiveness through Christ and those which have no such power."

Luther believed in justification—getting right with God—by faith alone. Now, St. Paul does teach justification by faith, but the key question is: What did St. Paul mean by the word *faith*? Luther thought it meant the confidence that the merits of Christ have been applied to one's personal account, or taking Christ as one's personal Savior. From then on, so long as a man continued to believe that point, he would be saved.

Actually, as scholarly Protestants today admit, this is not what St. Paul meant by faith. St. Paul meant by faith a total adherence of a man to God, so that if God speaks a truth, he believes; if God makes a promise, he is confident God will fulfill it; if God commands, he obeys. In this sense, the standard Protestant reference book *Interpreter's Dictionary of the Bible*, in its article "faith" in the latest supplementary volume (1976), says: "Paul uses *pistis/pisteuein* [Greek for "faith/believe"] to mean, above all, belief in the Christ kerygma [preaching, proclamation], knowledge, obedience, trust in the Lord Jesus. It comes by hearing with faith the gospel message . . . by responding with a confession about Christ . . . and by the 'obedience of faith' . . . 'the obedience which faith is.'"

Luther thought a book that intensely preaches this doctrine was inspired, otherwise not. Of course, he never provided proof for such a standard. Nor could it be a standard, for Luther, or any good writer, could compose a book that would preach according to Luther's requirements; yet that book need not on that account be inspired.

So Luther's attempt failed. Professor Smith adds that Luther "never applied this test minutely or critically." Such an application really could not be made.

John Calvin, in his *Institutes*, book 1, chapter vii, as cited by Professor Smith, offers a different test: "The word will never gain credit [belief] in the hearts of men till it be confirmed by the internal testimony of the Spirit. . . ." But Calvin's claim was too open to imagination and could never strictly prove anything. Smith's comment is devastating:

"The application of this test . . . would eliminate the existing distinction between canonical and noncanonical [inspired and noninspired] writings more completely than would the most radical conclusions of biblical criticism." Smith goes on to point out parts of Scripture that do not seem very spiritually uplifting to us today.

At this point, Professor Smith is about ready to give up and admit that there is no way to determine which books are inspired. "What about other tests . . .?" he asks. "Can we, for example, say that the Bible is infallible, while other books are fallible? Nothing is more noticeable than the gradual disappearance of that word 'infallible' from present-day theologies." And he goes on to point out what he considers errors in Scripture.

What Professor Smith demonstrates is that for a Protestant there simply is no way to know which books are inspired. That means, in practice, that a Protestant, if he is logical, should not appeal to Scripture to prove anything; he has no sure means of knowing which books are part of Scripture!

Smith's article appeared in 1911. A much more recent Protestant attempt really ends up in a vicious circle. Gerhard Maier, in *The End of the Historical-Critical Method*,[1] writes "only Scripture itself can say in a binding way what authority it claims and has. . . . We must let revelation determine its own limits. Consequently revelation defines itself. . . . Scripture considers itself as revelation" (pp. 61 and 63).

In other words, inspired Scripture is inspired because inspired Scripture says it is inspired Scripture.

There is really only one way to accomplish what we are asking for: let the Church decide which books are inspired. Professor Smith dismisses that approach as one that holds only if one believes in the authority of the Catholic Church. Of course, he did not.

Let us pursue this method, taking great pains lest we, too, find ourselves in the vicious circle of proving the authority of the Church by inspired Scripture, and proving the inspiration of Scripture by the Church.

Let us use the method of looking upon the Gospels, not as inspired books, but simply as documents from ancient times, works on a par with those of writers such as Caesar, Tacitus, Thucydides, and others.

First, with the help of the science of textual criticism, we check to see if our copies are at least substantially the same as the originals. This is needed since our oldest manuscripts are separated from the originals

11

by about three centuries. But that is no great problem. There is a gap of nine hundred to a thousand years between Caesar's original and our earliest manuscripts. Further, we can partly bridge the gap in the case of the Gospels by using translations that go back to within about a hundred years of the originals. These translations were made independently of each other, into several languages, in different parts of the Mediterranean world. Still further, the variants—differences in readings in different manuscripts—that we find are mostly trifling, and do not affect at all the six points that will be discussed shortly.

What literary pattern did the Gospel writers intend to use? It is clear that they intended to give facts about Jesus as a basis for faith. They had access to the facts, even if we take the latest dates proposed today for the first three Gospels 80-90 A.D. Many people in their sixties who had seen and heard Jesus himself would have been alive at that time. And Quadratus, an early apologist writing about 123 A.D., tells us that in his day there were still persons around who had been cured or raised from the dead by Jesus—prime witnesses![2]

The Gospel writers had the opportunity to get the facts. And we know that they would be careful and honest, for their own eternity depended on facts, not on fancy. As St. Paul told the Corinthians, "If Christ is not risen, your faith is vain" (1, 15:17). Or think of St. Ignatius of Antioch, who was eaten alive by beasts in Rome in about 107 A.D. He wanted to be eaten, to be more like Christ! If anyone thinks that he was indulging in fancies, let him take a copy of the letter of Ignatius to the Romans and stand by the lion cage in a zoo and read it!

We need to examine the first three Gospels, the Synoptics, for just six facts—facts that are not entangled with ancient cultural patterns, which would make it necessary for us to reconstruct those patterns. No, what we need are things the original onlookers could easily observe and accurately report.

Fact 1:   There was a man called Jesus.
Fact 2:   He claimed to be a messenger sent by God.
Fact 3:   He did enough to prove that He was such a messenger.

Now the mere fact of working miracles would not prove that Jesus was a messenger sent from God. It is probable that God at times worked miracles even for good pagans. But Jesus often appealed to His miracles as proof of His mission and teaching (see, among these, Matthew 11:2-5,

12

Luke 7:20-22, Mark 2:9-11). Now God is the ultimate source of the miraculous power; but He, being Truth, cannot provide such power as proof of a falsehood. So Jesus' claims were proved true. In fact, He proved that He could even forgive sins. A most remarkable messenger!

Many of Jesus' miracles could not be explained away as being the result of suggestion. No suggestion will multiply loaves and fishes or cure a man who was born blind. There is a hysterical kind of blindness that can come on later in life, which can be cured by suggestion. Nor would suggestion call out from the tomb a man dead for four days. And there have been many modern miracles, for example at Lourdes, that have been checked to the hilt by science. These miracles are in continuity with His miracles. Often they occur during the procession of the Blessed Sacrament, thus showing His Real Presence there. The Real Presence is proclaimed only by the Catholic Church, through continuity of ordination, going all the way back to Jesus Himself.

Fact 4:   Crowds followed Christ. But He had an inner circle to whom He spoke more intimately. This is merely what we would expect.

Fact 5:   He told His followers to continue His teaching.

Fact 6:   Jesus gave the message that God would protect that teaching: "He who hears you hears me; he who rejects you rejects me, and he who rejects me rejects him who sent me" (Luke 10:16).

In summary then, we see a group that is commissioned to teach by a messenger sent by God, and promised God's protection for that teaching. These observations are made without treating the Scriptures as inspired. Now we not only intellectually may but are intellectually driven to believe what the body teaches. That body can then assure us that those ancient documents, used without knowing they are inspired, really have God as their author. And that body, the Church, can also tell us that the messenger sent by God is really God Himself. And, of course, it can guarantee countless other truths for us.

It is true, the Gospels seldom use the word *church*. But the reality is important, not the word. We have seen that there is a body commissioned to teach, and that is all we need.

We should add this: As we will see in chapters 20-23, many critics think there is a gap between what Jesus was (Jesus of history) and what the early Church said He was (Christ of faith). They say it is not possible to know much on the early side of that gap. We reply: First, they ignore the fact that information was available on Jesus, as we saw in the above sketch, and that getting the basic facts right was vital to the eternity of each one. Hence the assumption of neither care nor knowledge is false. Secondly, we have a bypass in the six facts we have just sketched. We need to establish only the above six points, all very simple and obvious. Then we can let that body, commissioned by God's messenger, tell us all we need to know about who Jesus really was.

So now we can fulfill what the First Epistle of St. Peter asks of us (1 Peter 3:15): "Always be prepared to make a defense to anyone who calls you to account for the hope that is in you."

Chapter 3

Multiple Authors

A problem arises from the special kinds of ideas people of the ancient Near East had about literary authorship. We today are very conscious of the rights of the author to his own work. No one would dare to change it and publish it under that author's name. Not so in the ancient Near East. Someone later might make modifications, and still later, more and more modifications might be made—all leaving the name of the original author in place. Hence the question: Can this fit with the doctrine of inspiration? And if so, how?

It is often charged that the Pontifical Biblical Commission, in its early decrees, was excessively restrictive and narrow. Not in this instance! The Commission was asked about this sort of point. The question was whether in the first five books of the Old Testament we absolutely must hold that Moses either wrote each and every thing with his own hand or dictated them to scribes. The Commission's answer, given on June 27, 1906, was no.

The Commission also examined the theory that says "that the work, conceived by [Moses] under divine inspiration, was entrusted to another or to several to be written . . . and that finally the work done in this way and approved by the same Moses as the leader and inspired author was published." The Commission found this theory was permissible.

So it is not necessary to hold that Moses himself wrote all of the first five books. He could have commissioned others to do the work, checking and approving it after they had finished. After all, the Pope today sometimes works in this way, assigning some writer to prepare a document for him according to his own instructions. Later the Pope will publish it as his own. He might not even find any need for revisions.

The Commission also raised this question: "Can it be admitted . . . that in so long a course of ages, some modification happened to [the Pentateuch], such as additions after the death of Moses by an inspired author or glosses and explanations injected into the text, or that certain words and forms were changed from an ancient form of the language into more recent language; and that defective readings can be attributed to the hands of scribes, about which we may investigate and judge according to the norms of criticism?" The reply was: "Yes, subject to the judgment of the Church."

There is all the latitude one might desire. In dealing with the specific case of the Pentateuch, the first five books of the Old Testament, it is legitimate to think that Moses had others do part of the work, subject to his approval. We may also say that long after his death some other inspired author changed things that Moses had written or approved. The final touches would, obviously, had to have been done by an inspired author.

The Pontifical Biblical Commission also admits that some later person, not necessarily inspired, might have updated the forms of the language. For every language, while it is living and spoken, changes. After some time persons who use that language may no longer understand easily some older expressions. That could have happened to the Pentateuch, and someone might later have put the same ideas into more current language.

Behind all of these questions, lies the belief that Moses is in some way the author of the Pentateuch. That view can still be honestly maintained today. A highly respected recent Scripture scholar, Eugene Maly, writing in *The Jerome Biblical Commentary*, said: "Moses . . . is at the heart of the Pentateuch and can, in accord with the common acceptance of the ancient period, correctly be called its author" (I, p. 5, par. 24). In speaking of the "common acceptance of the ancient period," Father Maly has in mind precisely that, later on, persons often felt free to modify earlier writings while leaving the name of the original author on them.

So, in the case of many hands or authors, there could be several inspired authors; that is, each one who worked on a book could be inspired. But it is obviously also possible that in some cases only the final writer was inspired. In that case, one needs to approach the problem by way of literary genres to determine what to say about authors other than the final author. That approach will be explained in chapter 9.

But what about the sources that Moses might have used? The Pontifical Biblical Commission raised this question: "Can it be admitted, without prejudice to the Mosaic authorship of the Pentateuch, that Moses, in producing his work, used sources, that is, written documents or oral traditions, out of which, according to the special purpose he had in mind and under divine inspiration, he took some things and inserted them in his work word for word, or else substantially, while either enlarging or shortening them?" The answer was yes.

Behind this question lies the documentary theory of the Pentateuch. Really, the theory applies largely to the first four books: Genesis, Exodus, Leviticus, and Numbers. Deuteronomy is, to simplify a bit, still another source. For the first four books, it is usual to speak of three sources: J, for Yahwist; E, for Elohist; and P, for Priestly Code. It is customary to use the letter *J* to reflect the German spelling of *Yahweh*. Later hands, according to many scholars, modified the earlier work of Moses, utilizing these sources, some of which of course could stem from Moses himself or from different writers employed by him. J, the Yahwist, is so-called because of his fondness for using the word *Yahweh* for God, while the Elohist prefers *Elohim*. It is thought by many that the Yahwist furnished the outline and much of the content of those first four books. The Yahwist stresses events after the Patriarchs (Abraham, Isaac, and Jacob) as the fulfillment of the promises God made to these men. In a sense then, this could be called redemptive history.

The Elohist document is hard to separate from that of J, for both are early and primitive. E may have been a narrative from the Patriarchs to the generation that wandered in the Sinai Peninsula after receiving the Ten Commandments, while J is apt to use human terms—anthropomorphisms. For example, J speaks of God as angry and regretting that He had made man, or as coming down to see the tower of Babel. The Elohist is much less inclined to use anthropomorphisms. The third document, P, the Priestly Code, is noted for its concern for cultic things and religious laws. Thus the Book of Leviticus is entirely P.

Most scholars once agreed on the existence of these sources. Today that consensus has been seriously damaged, though very many do continue to hold the theory. Distinguished among those who do is Pope John Paul II, who in several of his many conferences on Genesis, speaks in a matter-of-fact way about these sources.[1] In speaking as he does, the

Pope was obviously not intending to impose this theory authoritatively on the whole Church. First, because it was only something he said in passing; second, because a question of authorship of books of Scripture is not a matter of revelation but of history. This is true even when the text of Scripture seems to identify an author. In that case, it should be recalled that the ancient concept of authorship differed from ours. Not only would later hands feel free to change things, but also a person might write a book using a pen name. And the pen name might be that of a famous personage. The Gospels of Mark and Luke, incidentally, are really by those men precisely because their names were not famous enough to tempt others to use them as pen names.

Impressive evidence against the documentary theory would appear if the claims of Giovanni Pettinato about discoveries in the buried City of Ebla can be substantiated. He claims that the divine names El and Yahweh were both known and used around 2500 B.C., and that he has found a creation account at Ebla very similar to that of Genesis. At present, there is immense controversy over these matters. Ebla was discovered in 1974-1975, in Syria. Over fifteen thousand clay tablets were found there, dating to around 2500 B.C.

Another remarkable case against the theory comes from a computer study made at the Technion Institute in Israel. The twenty thousand words of Genesis, in Hebrew, were fed into a computer programmed to make a thorough linguistic analysis of words, phrases, and passages in the text. The project coordinator, Yehuda Radday, reached a controversial conclusion: "It is most probable that the Book of Genesis was written by one person" (*Newsweek*, September 28, 1981, p. 59).

The debate is apt to rage for a long time before general agreement is reached. Meanwhile, we know that such a theory is possible, and that it will not conflict with the doctrine of inspiration, or even with Mosaic authorship of the Pentateuch.

Chapter 4

The Plural Senses of Scripture

As we saw, there can be more than one author of a book of Scripture. Can there be more than one literal sense of a scriptural passage? While we have no clear statement of the Church to guide us on this, it is quite possible according to very many scholars.

First, we need to clarify the expression "literal sense." It is not a crude, fundamentalistic way of understanding that treats the ancient writer as if he were a twentieth century American—as if one were to say: "Genesis speaks of six days. That means six times twenty-four hours." No, the literal sense is what the ancient writer really meant to convey. (More about such matters in chapter 9.)

To find what the ancient writer meant to convey, we must take into account differences of language. For example, our Lord tells us that we must hate our parents (Luke 14:26). Sadly, some cult leaders take this, unintelligently, as really meaning hate. Still more sadly, some of their duped young followers are even pleased to carry that hatred out. The truth is that our Lord would have been speaking either Aramaic or Hebrew—more likely the former. In either language, the degrees of comparison were missing. Where in English one would say, "Love me more, and them less," the Aramaic and Hebrew, lacking the right words, might say, "Love me and hate them."

We must also take into account the genre of literature the writer intends to produce. One writes differently in poetry, for example, than in prose.

There is also a *typical sense*, one in which there is what might be called a prophecy through actions instead of through words. For example, Isaac carrying the wood on which he was to be sacrificed is a forecast, a *type*, of Jesus carrying His cross. Since the existence of types depends on the will of God, we can be sure of that will only when a later part of Scripture tells us that about an earlier part, or when the Fathers or the Church tell us.

Sometimes scholars also speak of an *accommodative sense*. This is not really something intended by Scripture at all. It occurs when a speaker or writer applies the words of Scripture to something that they could fit but that was not intended by God or by the human author of Scripture.

There is no entirely clear statement by the Church on the possibility of more than one literal sense, which is called "fuller sense," or, using a Latin phrase, *sensus plenior*. We have only one text from Pope Leo XIII: "Since the author is the Holy Spirit, many things come under the words which far surpass the keen power of human reason, that is, divine mysteries, and many other things contained along with these. This [happens] sometimes with a fuller and more hidden meaning than that which the letter, and the laws of interpretation, seem to indicate" (*Providentissimus Deus*, 1893).

Yet, if we reflect that the Holy Spirit is the principal author of Scripture, it becomes obvious that He could intend to convey more by the words than the human author may have realized. Yes, the human author is sometimes described as an instrument that the transcendence of God uses. Yet that relationship should not bar God from intending more if He should so will. That additional meaning can become clear with the help of later parts of Scripture, or with the help of the Church.

Matthew 1:22-23 seems to be a case in point: "All this took place to fulfill what the Lord had spoken by the prophet: 'Behold, a virgin shall conceive and bear a son, and his name shall be called Emmanuel.'" St. Matthew is quoting Isaiah 7:14. The text of Isaiah has been discussed much by scholars. They have asked: Who is the child? What is the proper translation of *almah* here, which St. Matthew translates as "virgin"?

We first look at the setting. In 735 B.C., Syria (Aram) and Israel (the northern kingdom) invaded the southern kingdom of Judah to force King Achaz to join a coalition against Assyria. They really wanted to depose Achaz and set up a king of their own choosing. Achaz was tempted to join Assyria instead. Isaiah met the king, told him he must not do that,

that he must have faith. Isaiah promised him any sign he might ask for, but Achaz refused to ask. Isaiah was especially disturbed because to submit to Assyria would mean recognition of the god of Assyria (see 2 Kings 16). Isaiah promised the sign of the child to be born of the *almah*.

Most scholars today try to see this child as Hezekiah, son of Achaz. His birth would have been a sign within the lifetime of Achaz—an important point. The child would be a sign of one to continue the Davidic line. In favor of this view, it is pointed out that *almah* in Hebrew means simply "a young woman," presumably unmarried. It does not mean "a virgin." So the *almah* would be the wife of Achaz in this view.

But there are strong reasons for the view that the Holy Spirit, and perhaps also Isaiah, intended the virgin birth of Jesus. It is admitted that the child in Isaiah 7:14 is the same as the marvelous child of Isaiah 9:6 who is to be called "Wonderful Counsellor, Mighty God, Everlasting Father, Prince of Peace. Of the increase of his government and of peace there will be no end." Such a description hardly fits Hezekiah, even though he was a good king. Further, *almah* in the Hebrew text has the article *the*—which would be strange if it refers to the wife of Achaz. And again, that word is not very apt for a wife. Still further, the old Greek translation of the Old Testament, made in the third and second centuries B.C., uses *parthenos* ("virgin") for *almah*.

We can get some help, too, from the Targum on Isaiah 9:5-6. The Targums are ancient Aramaic translations plus comment, of the Old Testament. Their date is uncertain. Some think the Targum Jonathan on the prophets very early, pre-Christian; others would make it later. Whatever its date, it gives us an ancient Jewish understanding of the text, an understanding not helped by the hindsight of seeing it fulfilled in Jesus.

Now the Targum of Isaiah 9:5-6 sees the child as the Messiah. The same Targum on Isaiah 7:14 does not speak of that verse as Messianic, yet since it is generally admitted that the child of 9:5 is the same as the child of 7:14, the Targum implicitly recognizes the child of 7:14 as the Messiah and, therefore, not as Hezekiah.

There are, then, powerful reasons for saying that the understanding given us by St. Matthew is not just an accommodative sense but a fuller sense. Or, we could consider it as an instance of multiple fulfillment of a prophecy.

This situation is similar to Matthew 2:15: "This was to fulfill what the Lord had spoken by the prophet: 'Out of Egypt have I called my son.'" St. Matthew is making Hosea 11:1 refer to the return of the infant Jesus from Egypt. Yet, and St. Matthew would know it even better than we, Hosea 11:1 seems to speak of the Exodus of the Jews from Egypt under Moses; the son is the whole people of Israel. But again, we do not think St. Matthew meant this as a mere accommodative sense. It is a fuller sense or, alternatively, another case of multiple fulfillment of a prophecy. (These two possibilities often coincide.)

Genesis 3:15 is much discussed. In it God, after the fall of Adam and Eve, says to the tempter serpent: "I will put enmity between you and the woman, and between your seed and her seed." Some wish to argue that the only woman on the scene is Eve. Yet this view cannot explain how there is a permanent enmity between Eve and the tempter, to whom she has just fallen. And that her offspring is to conquer the serpent is hardly true of the descendants of Eve in general.

Some would retort that the Hebrew *shuf* is used to mean both that the serpent will "strike at" her heel and that the offspring of the woman will "strike at" the serpent's head. However, here again those three Targums help us. The ancient Targumists, knowing full well the meaning of the Hebrew, still not only made the verse Messianic but also saw in it a victory for the sons of the woman.

The result is that we too can see a fuller sense in Genesis 3:15. It predicts the victory of the offspring of the woman. The woman is Mary; her offspring, Jesus. A note on this verse in the New American Bible seems to understand this interpretation as at least possible. Far more important, Pope Pius XII, in the Encyclical "*Fulgens Corona Gloriae* (September 8, 1953), wrote: "The foundation [of the doctrine of the Immaculate Conception] is seen in the very Sacred Scripture in which God . . ., after the wretched fall of Adam, addressed the . . . serpent in these words . . .,'I will put enmity between you and the woman.'"

Now if the Immaculate Conception can be found in Genesis 3:15, so can Mary, the Immaculate one.

There are, of course, many other instances of the fuller sense. The topic of our next chapter, multiple fulfillment, will provide instances that can be considered fuller sense at the same time. Let us round off this chapter with a fascinating case of what seems to be a fuller sense in a work of a Father of the Church, St. Irenaeus, the martyr-bishop of Lyons, who died around 200 A.D.

In his work *Against Heresies* (3.22.4), St. Irenaeus brings out the parallel, in reverse, between Mary and the old Eve. Vatican II quotes it

22

this way: "Rightly then do the Holy Fathers look on Mary as not just passively employed by God but as freely cooperating in faith and obedience in human salvation. For she, as St. Irenaeus says, 'by obeying, became a cause of salvation for herself and for the whole human race'" (*Constitution on the Church*, n. 56).

Further on in the same section, St. Irenaeus adds this remarkable comparison: "For in no other way can that which is tied be untied, unless the very windings of the knot are gone through in reverse: so that the first joints are loosed through the second, and the second in turn free the first.   .   . . Thus then, the knot of the disobedience of Eve was untied through the obedience of Mary."

Now St. Irenaeus, in context, seems to be thinking of Mary's obedience on the day of the Annunciation. This was, of course, a cooperation in the Redemption. The Second Person of the Trinity could not die without a human nature. Mary, in furnishing that humanity, did share in the Redemption.

But did her cooperation cease there? Or did it extend even to taking part in the great sacrifice itself? The comparison of the knot implies that she shared even in Calvary; for it was only then, and not earlier, that the knot really was untied.

Did St. Irenaeus see all the implications of his own words? If he did, he did not show it. But Vatican II, as we saw, quoted St. Irenaeus, adding: "In suffering with Him as He died on the cross, she cooperated in the work of the Savior, in an altogether singular way, by obedience, faith, hope and burning love, to restore supernatural life to souls. As a result, she is our Mother in the order of grace" (n. 61).

St. Irenaeus probably did not see the full implication. Yet he, a Father of the Church, was an instrument in the hand of Divine Providence. That same Divine Providence led Vatican II to see what St. Irenaeus had not seen in his own words.

Similarly, the human writers of Scripture may not have seen all that the Holy Spirit intended through their words. The Church later would see these things.

Chapter 5

Multiple Fulfillment

A remarkable phenomenon appears in a number of places in Scripture. Oddly, it has been little noticed by scholars. It seems that prophecies can have more than one fulfillment.

Second Timothy 3 opens by saying: "But understand this, that in the last days there will come times of stress. For men will be lovers of self, lovers of money, proud, arrogant, abusive, disobedient to their parents, ungrateful, unholy, inhuman, implacable, slanderers, profligates, fierce. . . ." And the dreadful litany continues. (Incidentally, the picture given here of the time just before the end is as opposite as it can be to the dreams of Teilhard de Chardin, who taught that just before the return of Christ, most of the world would be bound together in close love, and perhaps also telepathy. Compare also Luke 18:8, Matthew 24:12, and 2 Thessalonians 2:3.)

The Jerome Biblical Commentary, on that passage in 2 Timothy, observes: "*In the last days*: in the Messianic period, but with special emphasis here on the final days before the parousia [the return of Christ at the end]." "The last days" has a double meaning: it refers to all the time between the Ascension and the return of Jesus, and also to the time just before that return. Notice that the whole time from Ascension to end is called "the last days." The reason is that we are now in the final period of God's dealings with men. There is to be no other arrangement or regime to supplant Christianity. (On this, compare Vatican Council II, *Constitution on Divine Revelation*, n. 4.) This helps us understand some

otherwise puzzling words in Scripture, in which we are told that the time
is short (including 1 Corinthians 7:29, Revelation 1:3, and 2 Peter 3:8,
wherein we read that "with the Lord one day is as a thousand years, and
a thousand years as one day").

Another fascinating instance is found in the prophet Daniel 12:7.
The man clothed in linen who has appeared to Daniel raises his right
hand and his left to the sky and swears by Him who lives forever "that it
would be for a time, two times, and a half a time; and that when the
shattering of the power of the holy people comes to an end all these
things would be accomplished." A note in the New American Bible on
Daniel 12:7 explains the three and a half years as either a symbol of evil
(half of seven, the perfect number) or as the total approximate duration
of the persecution of the Jews by Antiochus Epiphanes of Syria. "The
author's perspective," the note adds, "is the end of Antiochus, and beyond, the final consummation of all things." Again it is shown that a
prophecy may have more than one fulfillment.

Incidentally, the translation of the words of Daniel 12:7 saying
that the things will happen "when the shattering of the power of the holy
people comes to an end" is much debated. Some commentators have
even gone so far as to suggest that we are here dealing with a mistransla-
tion into Hebrew from an Aramaic original (see Anchor Bible, p. 274).
In the next verse, Daniel 12:8, Daniel himself is also puzzled: "I heard
but I did not understand." Most scholars seem not to have noted another
possible translation of the Hebrew *ukekalloth* in verse 7. The expression
would then read that these things will happen—in the final fulfillment of
the prophecy—"when He has brought to an end (completed) the scatter-
ing of the power of the holy people." This could conceivably refer to the
final reunion of the scattered Israelites from the dispersion.

The interpretations of St. Matthew's Gospel of Isaiah 7:14 and
Hosea 11:1, which we offered as probable instances of a fuller or multiple literal sense, can also, obviously, be taken as instances of multiple
fulfillment of prophecies.

A specially interesting probable case of multiple fulfillment comes
in the mysterious chapter 24 of St. Matthew. At the start, the disciples
ask Jesus for the signs of two things: the fall of Jerusalem, and of the
end of the world. Commentators are far from agreement on interpreting
the rest of the chapter. Some have tried to divide it so as to have parts
refer to one question, others to the other. But a careful analysis reveals

that practically all of the signs given were actually fulfilled before the fall of Jerusalem in 70 A.D.

Jesus first warns: "For many will come in my name, saying, 'I am the Christ,' and they will lead many astray." There were false Messiahs before 70 A.D. The Acts of the Apostles 5:36-37 tells of revolts led by self-proclaimed Messiahs named Theudas and Judas of Galilee. There is a problem as to the dates of these Messiahs. Judas seems to belong to 6-7 A.D., but his followers were probably active long after that. Gamaliel is represented in Acts as saying that Theudas was recent, that is, in the 30s, while Josephus, a later Jewish historian, places Theudas in the 40s. But Josephus is not always accurate, and Luke may be using the Greek genre of speeches within history. (See chapter 9.) Acts 21:38 speaks of another such leader from Egypt without giving his name.

Of course there will be false Messiahs before the end: the great Antichrist himself, and lesser figures claiming to be Christ.

Jesus continued: "And you will hear of wars and rumors of wars. . . . There will be famines and earthquakes in various places: all this is but the beginning of the sufferings."

There were many wars before 70 A.D. Besides the smaller struggles over false Messiahs, there was the great Jewish revolt that began in 66 A.D. Further, in 69 A.D. the Roman empire suffered, after the fall of Nero, from what is called the year of the four emperors: Galba, Otho, Vitellius, and Vespasian. The first three held power only for a few months each. There were famines in the time of Emperor Claudius, who ruled from 41-54 A.D. The Acts of the Apostles 11:28 says that a prophet, Agabus, predicted a severe famine.

There were pestilences too. The Roman historian Tacitus, in *Annals* 16:13, says of the year 65 A.D.: "A year of shame and of so many evil deeds, heaven also marked by storms and pestilence. Campania was devastated by a hurricane, which destroyed everywhere country houses, plantations and crops, and carried its rage to the neighborhood of Rome, where a dreadful plague was sweeping away all classes of human beings. . . . The houses were filled with lifeless bodies, and the streets with funerals. No age or sex was spared. Slaves and freeborn were cut off alike. . . . Knights and senators died indiscriminately."

Tacitus also reports many earthquakes in various places in the empire: in the province of Asia in 53 A.D. (*Annals* 12:58), frequent shocks in Rome itself in 51 A.D. (*Annals* 12:43), in Campania and especially Pompeii in 62 A.D. (*Annals* 15:22). The Roman philosopher Seneca and the Jewish historian Josephus also report earthquakes.

Jesus also foretold persecution: "Then they will deliver you up to tribulation, and put you to death: and you will be hated by all nations for my name's sake. And then many will fall away, and betray one another, and hate one another" (Matthew 24:9-10).

There is no need to cite the documentation for persecutions before 70 A.D. The facts are too well known. The Second Epistle to Timothy adds: "Indeed all who desire to live a godly life in Christ Jesus will be persecuted" (3:12). Before the final end, "Also it [the Beast, the Antichrist] causes all, both small and great, both rich and poor, both free and slave, to be marked on the right hand or the forehead, so that no one can buy or sell unless he has the mark, that is, the name of the beast, or the number of its name" (Revelation 13:16;17).

The next words of Jesus in Matthew are frightening: "And because wickedness is multiplied most men's love will grow cold" (24:12). None of the usual translations really brings out fully the complete force of the Greek for the first words of this line, for English does not have the needed structure. Freely, it means: "Because sin will go the limit, the love of most people will grow cold." (What a contrast to the dream of Teilhard de Chardin!)

We think too of the terrible warning given by Jesus in Luke: "When the Son of man comes, will he find faith on earth?" (18:8). We do not have a record of so great an apostasy before 70 A.D. But there was immense sin. Perhaps we should just say that the multiple fulfillment is not total in all details.

Matthew predicts that "this gospel of the kingdom will be preached throughout the whole world, as a testimony to all nations; and then the end will come" (24:14). The language is well adapted to multiple fulfillment, for the Gospel was indeed preached throughout most of the Mediterranean world before the fall of Jerusalem. St. Paul himself told the Romans (15:23) that he no longer had a place to preach in the eastern Mediterranean. Before the ultimate end, the Gospel will reach absolutely all parts of the globe.

A difficult line follows in the next verse of Matthew: "So when you see the desolating sacrilege spoken of by the prophet Daniel, standing in the holy place . . . then let those who are in Judea flee to the mountains" (24:15).

Daniel referred to the desecration of the Temple in the persecution of Antiochus Epiphanes (167-165 B.C.). THe Roman Emperor Caligula, in 40 A.D., ordered that a statue be placed in the Jerusalem Temple. It seems that his subordinates had the good judgment to ignore the command. However, as the earliest Church historian, Eusebius, tells us (*History*, 3.5), many Christians in Jerusalem did see something that led them to flee the city of Pella before the fall of Jerusalem. Did they merely see the course of events developing? Or did they actually see the eagles atop the standards of Roman soldiers in the outer temple area? The soldiers actually worshiped those eagles, so they were literally idols.

"Immediately after the tribulation of those days," Matthew warns, "the sun will be darkened, and the moon will not give its light, and the stars will fall from heaven, and the powers of the heavens will be shaken; then will appear the sign of the Son of man in heaven" (24:29-31).

We might say that these words apply only to the final end. Yet they seem to be an odd pattern of writing, called apocalyptic, that arose in Judaism around the second century B.C. and had a run of about four centuries. This kind of writing uses extremely colorful imagery, much stronger than a sober description would call for. Thus in Isaiah, referring to the fall of Babylon, we find: "Behold, the day of the Lord comes, cruel with wrath and fierce anger, to make the earth a desolation. . . . For the stars of the heavens and their constellations will not give their light; the sun will be dark at its rising and the moon will not shed its light" (13:9-10). (Compare Isaiah 34:4, on the fall of Edom, and Ezekiel 32:7-8, on the distress coming to Egypt.)

Finally Jesus Himself warns us that the signs are not so clear that most people will read them: "As were the days of Noah, so will be the coming of the Son of man" (Matthew 24:37). People will be eating, drinking, marrying—business as usual. And suddenly it will be there, the visitation (the concept of the Hebrew *paqad:* God coming to "visit" for weal or woe). Hence St. Paul told the Thessalonians that the day would come "like a thief in the night" (1,5:2-3; compare also 2 Peter 3:10 and Matthew 24:36-44).

What of the words "Truly, I say to you, this generation will not pass away till all these things take place" (Matthew 24:34)? These words came true most clearly in that many of the original hearers of Jesus were alive in 70 A.D. But the words can also refer to the final end. As Vatican II tells us, Christianity is the final stage of God's dealings with man. It will not be supplanted by another regime. So the Christian dispensation, the Messianic Age, will not pass away before the end (*On Divine Revelation*, par. 4).

Interestingly, St. Augustine often makes use of the technique similar to our multiple-fulfillment idea in his great *City of God*. He studies minutely an Old Testament prophecy, such as that in 2 Samuel 7:8-16 or Psalm 72. Following a translation that matches the Vulgate, St. Augustine noted that the promise to David that his successor would build a Temple was not entirely fulfilled in Solomon, since verse 16, as St. Augustine read it, said: "His house will be faithful." But Solomon was not faithful; he fell into idolatry. So the prophecy, which partly fits Solomon, completely fits Christ. He and His house, the Church, will always be faithful, will last forever. (Other examples in St. Augustine's *City of God* are 17:13 and 18:45.)

Finally the monks of Qumran, writers of the Dead Sea Scrolls, seem to have had similar ideas, as can be seen in their *pesher* commentary on the prophet Habakkuk. They "update" the message to refer to their own community.

Chapter 6

Inspiration and Inerrancy— General

Since God is the principal author of Holy Scripture, it follows that Scripture can contain absolutely no error of any kind.

Yet today there are numerous charges of error in Scripture, even from Catholics. They often begin by confusing the issue with terminology. They say that there are two ways of looking at the question, *a prior*, and *a posteriori*. If we look a priori, that is in advance of checking the text of Scripture, we say, "God is the author; therefore no error is possible." But these people say, "Let us look a posteriori, that is, let us consider the question *after* looking at the text." When they do that, they say, in effect: "Look at all the errors we found in Scripture! Since there are errors, of course there can be errors!"

A strong example of this new position is provided by Thomas A. Hoffman, S.J.[1] As essential for the sacred character of Scripture, Hoffman requires that the writings be: "(1) *inspired*, that is originating from and communicating the Spirit of God; (2) in some sense *normative* for the community; and (3) *canonical*, having official and unique authoritative status."

At first sight, Hoffman's criteria seem to be in accord with the Church. But we need a closer look. As to inspiration, Hoffman says, "I maintain that what they meant was simply a writing in which they experienced the power, truth, etc., of the Spirit of Christ. . . ." But this is really subjective and does not at all imply freedom from error. Hence,

31

Father Hoffman adds, "The term *inerrancy* is dropped in this paper as having no positive theological contribution to make." Father Hoffman says this because he uses the *a posteriori* approach. He looks at the text and judges it to be so full of errors that to try to explain them away is "basically patching holes on a sinking ship."

To try to defend Scripture against charges of error, Father Hoffman adds, shows a lack of faith. "What is at work here is a search for a security that is not only nonexistent but incompatible with the total dependence upon the faith-covenant that is at the heart of Judeo-Christian religion, a kind of idolatry that gives a certitude that trespasses upon the true Christian faith-relationship with God."

At first sight, these words may seem a strong expression of faith. Actually, they deprive faith of its basis. "Believe because you will to believe," is what they are saying. Neither the Catholic Church nor Holy Scripture takes such an attitude. Thus the First Epistle of St. Peter admonishes us: "Always be prepared to make a defense to anyone who calls you to account for the hope that is in you . . ." (3:15).

As we saw in chapter 2, there is a solid, rational process that starts by regarding the Gospels merely as ancient documents and moves forward to prove the teaching commission of the Church, given to it by a Messenger sent by God, who has promised it His protection.

The situation becomes clearer when we compare the proposal of Father Hoffman to that of Rudolph Bultmann, father of "form criticism."[2] Bultmann's contention is that faith cannot be logically proven. "The man who wishes to believe in God as his God," says Bultmann, "must realize that he has nothing in his hand on which to base his faith. He is suspended in mid-air, and cannot demand a proof of the word which addresses him. . . . Security can be found only by abandoning all security."

If Bultmann meant that we should first arrive at the divinity of Jesus, the Divine Word, and then without further question believe Him, that would be splendid. But he does not mean that at all. Thinking that we can know hardly anything with certitude about Jesus, Bultmann reinterprets the Gospels to make them mean the same as a bizarre modern German existentialist, Martin Heidegger.[3] Bultmann says that his "demythologizing" of the New Testament (making it mean the same as Heidegger and removing the myths) is "in fact a perfect parallel to St. Paul's and Luther's doctrine of justification by faith alone. . . . It destroys every false security," of trying to work to a rational preliminary to faith. Just as in justification by faith, we have no basis in works, so in faith we have no basis in rational preliminaries. Bultmann goes still further: "The old quest for visible security, the hankering after tangible realities . . . is sin. . . . Faith means turning our backs on self and abandoning all security."[4]

In short, the proposals of Father Hoffman and Bultmann remind us of the desire of the Danish existentialist Kierkegaard to make faith just "a leap." We, as it were, jump up to Cloud 9, and believe because we decide to believe. We must not be prepared, as St. Peter wishes, to "have an answer ready for people who ask you the reason for the hope you have." We are reminded of St. Paul's warning in 2 Corinthians 11:13-14: "Such men are false apostles. They practice deceit in their disguise as apostles of Christ. And little wonder! For even Satan disguises himself as an angel of light."

There are many others who, like Father Hoffman, keep on insisting that there *are* errors in Scripture, in spite of the teaching of the Church that God is the chief author. They change the meaning of the word inspiration. An inspired writing, they say, is one in which one experiences the power and truth of the Spirit.[5] But we ask: How does this differ from the Protestant theory invented by Calvin (see chapter 2), that we know a book is inspired when the Spirit tells each one, interiorly, that it is inspired?

Oddly these claims of errors are made precisely at a time when the new techniques of Scripture study make it possible to answer these claims of errors. We will show in detail how to do that in this book, whose very title tells us that Scripture really is *Free From All Error.*

Before getting into the specifics, we should see on the positive side and in general what the Catholic Church teaches about inerrancy in Scripture. We already saw that Vatican Council I taught that the books of Scripture are sacred, not only because "they contain revelation without error, but because, since they were written by the inspiration of the Holy Spirit, they have God as their author."

Now it is completely obvious that if God is the author, there can be no error. Pius XII, in his Encyclical on Scripture, *Divino Afflante Spiritu* (1943), after quoting this statement of Vatican I, commented: "In our age, the Vatican Council, to reject false teachings about inspiration, declared that these same books [of Scripture] must be considered 'as sacred and canonical' by the Church, 'not only because they contain revelation without error, but because, being written by the inspiration of the Holy Spirit, they have God as their author, and as such have been handed down to the Church.'"

"But then," Pius XII adds, "when certain Catholic authors, contrary to this solemn definition of Catholic doctrine, in which authority of this kind is claimed which enjoys immunity from any error whatsoever, for these books 'whole and entire, with all their parts'—when these authors had dared to restrict the truth of Holy Scripture to matters of faith and morals . . . our Predecessor of Immortal memory, Leo XIII, in an encyclical, *Providentissimus Deus*, . . . rightly and properly refuted those errors. . . ."

Some writers had said that matters of natural science or history, or things said in passing, are not protected from inerrancy. Only things pertaining to faith and morals, they said, are so protected. Pius XII pointed out the obvious: that if God is the author, there can be no error whatsoever, of any kind. And he spoke of the teaching of Vatican I on this point as "a solemn definition." Authors such as Raymond Brown, for example, insist there can be errors, even in religious matters! The next chapter will consider these charges.

Correct method is vital in studying any matter. Failure to use proper method in science resulted in such scant progress, mixed with manifold errors, until rather recent times. When scientists switched to the right method, the result was the splendid explosion of progress that has not yet subsided.

The point concerning method to be made here is this: one must distinguish the *fact* from the *how*. The *fact* that there is no error in Scripture, we know from the teachings of the Church. But how to explain certain difficulties requires additional work. However, and this is the vital point, even if we were not able at present to find the *how* that will solve particular problems, that should not blind us to the *fact* that there is an answer. We know infallibly that there is an answer, from the Church's teaching that there is no error. Moreover, there can be no error whatsoever in Scripture, precisely because the principal author of Scripture is God Himself.

Today, thanks to new techniques in the study of Scripture, we can solve numerous problems that utterly baffled scholars even as recently as the early part of this century. These earlier scholars, both Catholic and Protestant, knew how to solve some problems in Scripture, but they were well aware they could not solve certain others. Yet because they were persons of excellent faith, they knew that every difficulty must have an answer, even if they couldn't find it.

Today, incomprehensibly, we have the reverse situation. Precisely at the time when new techniques enable us to do what seemed impossible before, so many scholars are not only not solving the problems but even saying that problems are insoluble whose answers have been known for a long time! For example, Joseph Fitzmyer, S.J., notes two seeming contradictions in the three accounts of the conversion of St. Paul, in Acts 9:3-19, 22:6-16, and 26:12-18.[6]

In one account of Paul's conversion, his companions heard the voice that spoke to him; in another they did not. In one account, Paul's companions were thrown to the ground; in the other, they stood amazed. Fitzmyer says that "the variants may be due to the different sources of Luke's information." But these difficulties have been resolved for a long time. As to the question about hearing vs not hearing, the explanation lies in the meaning of the Greek *akouein,* which signifies either to know that there is a sound or to understand what it says. A case of hearing a sound without knowing what it says is found in John 12:29, where a voice from the sky speaks to Jesus. He understands, but people in the crowd thought that they had heard thunder.

As to the second problem, if one is literally knocked off his feet by such an experience, he will in a moment scramble to his feet and then stand and look puzzled.

Chapter 7

Scriptural Inerrancy in Science and Religion

Inspiration rules out any sort of error in the Bible whatsoever. Thus Pope Leo XIII, in his Encyclical *Providentissimus Deus,* wrote that since God is the author, "it follows that they who think any error is contained in the authentic passages of the Sacred Books surely either pervert the Catholic notion of divine inspiration, or make God Himself the source of error." Note that Pope Leo said that one of two things happens: either they pervert the notion of inspiration, or they make God the author of error.

Charges of error refer primarily to three fields today, matters of science, of religion, or of history. We will take up each of these in detail, putting off the matters of history until after our chapter on literary genre.

We turn first to the matters of natural science. Some assert that Pope Leo XIII, in his Encyclical on Scripture, *Providentissimus Deus,* which appeared in 1893,[1] took an indirect way of admitting that Scripture contains errors in the matters of natural science, when he said that statements made about natural things according to appearances are not errors.

Here is what Leo XIII actually said: "We must first consider that the sacred writers, or, more truly, 'the Spirit of God, who spoke through them,' did not will to teach these things (that is, the inner constitution of visible things) which were of no use for salvation, wherefore they at

37

times described things . . . as the common way of speaking at the time they did."

To try to say Leo XIII was indirectly admitting errors is very foolish. After all, we still today speak of the sun as rising and setting, though we know perfectly well that it does not do so. It is the earth that moves. Who would say that we are involved in habitual error on this account?

When we turn to the question of other kinds of errors, we meet a very common and bold challenge. Many today claim that Vatican II, in its *Constitution on Divine Revelation,* deliberately allowed us to say there can be errors of all kinds in Scripture, even religious errors! Only religious things that are needed for salvation would be free from error! The sentence of Vatican II that they appeal to is the following: "The books of Scripture must be acknowledged as teaching firmly, faithfully, and without error that truth *which God wanted put into the sacred writings for the sake of our salvation.*"[2] We have added italics to mark out the critical words. The claim is made that this clause is *restrictive.* If so, it would mean that *only* those things which are for our salvation are free from all error. Actually, the clause is merely *descriptive,* not *restrictive.* We know this by many means. Among other things the theological commission at the Council, after many bitter debates on this very question, explained: "The expression *salutaris* [for the sake of salvation] should in no way imply that Scripture is not, in its totality, inspired and the word of God."[3]

The very language used in this line, in Latin, could have clearly marked the clause as restrictive by using in Latin the construction *qui . . . quidem* with the subjunctive. But that construction was not used.

But the most decisive proof of what Vatican II really meant in the sentence under consideration is this: Pope Pius XII in his great Encyclical, *Divino Afflante Spiritu* (1943), had quoted the words of Vatican I saying that God Himself is the chief author of Scripture, and commented that the words of Vatican I were "a solemn definition." Of course Vatican II would not contradict a solemn definition! That would be heresy. And no matter on what level Vatican II was teaching at this point, it could not possibly teach heresy. Really, Vatican II even added four footnotes to this very passage in which it refers us to the text mentioned of Vatican I and to several pages of Leo XIII's Encyclical, and to two passages of Pius XII—all of which insist more than once with great care that there is no error of any kind at all in Scripture.

38

Some today think they have found a clear example of error in Job 14:13-22, and in some passages of Sirach/Ecclesiasticus.

In Job 14:9-12, just before the lines in question, Job had said that although a tree may seem to die and then shoot up again, man when he falls, does not return. Job is merely denying a return to life as we know it. He does seem to know of some sort of resurrection (probably not a glorious one such as we know from the New Testament), as will be seen presently in Job 19:25-27. He means that no one leaves the tomb and rejoins family and community.

In verse 13, Job says: "Oh that thou wouldest hide me in Sheol, that thou wouldest conceal me until thy wrath be past, that thou wouldest appoint me a set time and remember me! If a man die, shall he live again?" Again, Job is denying a return to the present life. But after that, in high-flown poetry, Job is wishing, fancifully, that God would let him hide, alive, in Sheol, the abode of the dead, until God's anger would pass. Then Job might emerge again.

Job knows this is only a fancy, yet poets do indulge in fancy. So Marvin Pope, in his Anchor Bible commentary on Job, says, "If only God would grant him asylum in the nether world, safe from the wrath that now besets him, and then appoint a time for a new and sympathetic hearing, he would be willing to wait, or even to endure the present evil" (p. 102). Such fancies occur not only in Job's poetry; other places in Scripture provide similar thoughts. Marvin Pope adds: "Isaiah xxvi 20 calls ironically on the people of Judah to hide in their chambers till Yahweh's wrath be past, and Amos ix 2 ff. pictures the wicked as trying vainly to hide in Sheol, heaven, Mount Carmel, the bottom of the sea."

The text of Job continues the fancy he began in the previous lines: "All the days of my service I would wait, till my release should come. Thou wouldest call and I would answer thee; thou wouldest long for the work of thy hands." Then Job adds more on the state he enjoys dreaming of: "For then thou wouldest number my steps, thou wouldest not keep watch over my sin; my transgression would be sealed up in a bag, and thou wouldest cover over my iniquity."

Then Job pushes aside his fancy, knowing it is only a fancy: "But the mountain falls and crumbles away, and the rock is removed from its place; the waters wear away the stones; the torrents wash away the soil of the earth; so thou destroyest the hope of man. Thou prevailest for ever against him, and he passes; thou changest his countenance and sendest him away. "Job is saying here that nothing can hold out against

God. All go down into the grave and return no more to this life.

While the father is in Sheol, "his sons come to honor, and he does not know it; they are brought low and he perceives it not." Job is saying that when a man goes to Sheol he no longer knows what goes on upon the earth. Why? If a soul reaches the beatific vision, he will know all that pertains to him on earth. Without that vision, is there any means of knowing? Even today, we do not see any means, unless of course God chooses to reveal things to a soul in purgatory.

But—and this is of capital importance—conditions in the after-life were radically different in the day of Job from what they are today. Why? Jesus had not yet died. Heaven, the vision of God, was not open, even to the just who had paid in full the debt of their sins. Theologians commonly speak of this state as the Limbo of the Fathers.[4]

Job was quite right. In Sheol there is no knowledge of what goes on on earth. Since there is no such knowledge, "he feels no pain for anything but his own body, makes no lament, save for his own life." But those words do imply consciousness in Sheol.

Really, it would be strange if Job would have no knowledge of an afterlife. The Book of Job probably was composed between the seventh and fifth centuries B.C. Before that, in the eighth century, Isaiah 14:9-11 pictures the souls in Hades as taunting the fallen rulers of Babylon as they arrive. Isaiah 26:19 says: "Thy dead shall live, their bodies shall rise. O dwellers in the dust, awake and sing for joy! For thy dew is a dew of light, and on the land of the shades thou wilt let it fall."

The Jerome Biblical Commentary (1968) comments on the text of Isaiah 26:19: "There is an explicit hope in the resurrection of individuals" (I, p. 277). Of course, but not to the conditions of present life. Job denies a return to present conditions, and he does not seem to know of a *glorious* resurrection. Isaiah does not hint at glory.

Jesus Himself refuted the Sadducees by pointing out that Sheol does not mean annihilation. He reminded them that God had said to Moses, "I am the God of Abraham, and the God of Isaac, and the God of Jacob." Then Jesus added: "He is not God of the dead, but of the living . . ." (Mark 12:26-27).

In fact, though the sense of the passage is debated, many think that Job (19:25-27) does look ahead to a resurrection, even if not the glorious kind we know: "For I know that my Redeemer lives, and at last he will stand upon the earth, and after my skin has been thus destroyed, then from my flesh I shall see God." These lines cannot be taken to mean a rescue for Job in this life, for in 7:6-7 Job had given up on that: "My days are swifter than a weaver's shuttle, and come to their end without hope. Remember that my life is a breath; my eye will never again see good."

It should be recalled that the Hebrews spent centuries in Egypt, where there was a well-developed idea of the afterlife. Afterward they lived in Canaan among a people who also had such ideas. How could they fail to have an idea of an afterlife?

Some also like to claim there is a denial of an afterlife in Sirach, also called Ecclesiasticus. In 14:16-17 we read: "Give, and take and beguile yourself, because in Hades one cannot look for luxury." We already know the answer. The afterlife before the death of Christ was the dull Limbo of the Fathers, where they waited to enter the vision of God.

Unfortunately, not all versions use the same numberings for the verses of our next passage. What some call Sirach 17:22-23 is 17:27-28 in the Revised Standard Version: "Who will sing praises to the Most High in Hades, as do those who are alive and give thanks? From the dead, as from one who does not exist, thanksgiving has ceased." M. Dahood, in Anchor Bible commentary on Psalms 6:6 (6:5 in Revised Standard Version), has a similar thought: "The psalmist suffers not because of the inability to remember Yahweh in Sheol, but from being unable to share in the praise of Yahweh which characterizes Israel's worship."

Israelites loved the grand liturgical praises of God, but there is no such thing in the dull Limbo of the Fathers. Isaiah 38:18 has a similar thought: "For Sheol cannot thank thee, death cannot praise thee." The Hebrew for *extol* there is *hallel,* the same word that is used in 1 Chronicles 16:4 and 2 Chronicles 5:13, 31:2, for the *liturgical* praise of God.

Some also appeal to Sirach/Ecclesiasticus 38:21: "Do not forget, there is no coming back; you do the dead no good, and injure yourself." There is no "coming back," again, means that there is no return to the present form of life. So this verse, too, is no real problem and does not at all prove an error in Scripture.

Chapter 8

Charges of Religious Errors

Chapter 7 answered the strongest charges of religious error in Scripture that are being made today. There are other such charges. This chapter will discuss some major ones.

Let us turn to Ecclesiastes, also called Qoheleth, a book probably written around the third century B.C. In the opening line, the author calls himself "son of David, king in Jerusalem." However, just as we today sometimes use pen names, so did they, except that they were inclined to pick the name of a famous person. This book does mark an advance in the ideas of retribution, according to some commentators. But it presents special problems that need a special method to solve.

In divine matters, it is not strange to encounter two truths that seem to conflict. We should, of course, check to see if we have understood correctly. If we have, we need to be careful not to deny or force either of the truths. Everyone admits this point when it is stated in a general way; but when it comes to particular cases, too often it is forgotten.

Qoheleth is very faithful to this method. He knew that the good may suffer in this life, while the wicked may prosper; though at times both fare the same. He does not seem to have known clearly, at least the truth of retribution, reward and punishment in the future life, though we admit that careful study of Qoheleth could lead to either conclusion on this point.

The result is that we find two sets of statements in Qoheleth.

They are so different that some commentators, chiefly in the past, thought that the book must have had two authors.

The texts that seem not to know of future retribution include 2:14: "The wise man has eyes in his head, but the fool walks in darkness; and yet I perceived that one fate comes to all of them."

A similar idea is found in 3:19-21: "For the fate of the sons of men and fate of beasts is the same; as one dies, so dies the other. They all have the same breath, and man has no advantage over the beasts; for all is vanity. All go to the same place; all are from the dust and all turn to dust again. Who knows whether the spirit of man goes upward and the spirit of the beast goes down to the earth?"

Qoheleth writes that all turn to dust, man and beast alike, with no apparent difference. Yet there may be a hint here of something further for man: "Who knows whether the spirit of man goes upward?" The translation here is debated. Instead of *spirit*, the New American Bible renders it "life-breath."

An even stronger-sounding text is 9:5-6: "For the living know that they will die, but the dead know nothing, and they have no more reward; but the memory of them is lost. Their love and their hate and their envy have already perished, and they have no more for ever any share in all that is done under the sun." The dead are in the Limbo of the Fathers.

But none of these texts really denies an afterlife. They are to be balanced by those of the second series.

Chapter 3:17 says, "I said in my heart, God will judge the righteous and the wicked." But Qoheleth knows that justice is not always accomplished in this life. So there seems to be an implication that the next life will make it right. Similarly, 8:12-14 says: "Though a sinner does evil a hundred times and prolongs his life, yet I know it will be well with those who fear God. . . . There is a vanity which takes place on earth, that there are righteous men to whom it happens according to the deeds of the wicked, and there are wicked men to whom it happens according to the deeds of the righteous." The author could easily mean that things must be rectified in another life.

The same implication appears in 12:13-14: "The end of the matter; all has been heard. Fear God, and keep his commandments; for this is the whole duty of man. For God will bring every deed into judgment, with every secret thing, whether good or evil."

In 9:10 we get again the drab image of the Limbo of the Fathers:

"Whatever your hand finds to do, do it with your might; for there is no work or thought or knowledge or wisdom in Sheol, to which you are going."

We can easily see that Qoheleth faithfully reported both truths without seeing clearly how to reconcile them. Yet, objectively, everything he said was true if properly understood.

Wilfrid Harrington makes severe charges about the image of Mary given in Mark 3:31-35. He thinks that verses 31-35 refer to the same group of persons as those in verses 20-21, so that the Blessed Virgin Mary is meant in 31-35: "For Mark [3:31-35] is a continuation of vv. 20-21 . . . his own did not receive him."[1] Harrington seems to mean that Mary did not believe in Him, and even says that the passage "may be seen to distinguish those who stood outside the sphere of salvation, and those who are within it." This seems to mean she was "outside the sphere of salvation"! This, of course, would really clash with the picture given by Luke's Gospel, in which she is blessed for her believing from the very start. Of course one Evangelist does not contradict another Evangelist!

To follow this, we must review the two scenes, Mark 3:21 and 3:31. In 3:20-21, we read: "Then he went home; and the crowd came together again, so that they could not even eat. And when his friends heard it, they went out to seize him, for they said, 'He is beside himself.'" We notice the mention of his friends. Harrington thinks Mary was among them, and further, that it is the same group of people, including her, who appear ten verses later, in 3:31: "And his mother and his brethren came; and standing outside they sent to him and called him." He replied in 3:33-35: "Who are my mother and my brethren? . . . Whoever does the will of God is my brother, and sister, and mother."

Now of course we admit that each Evangelist wrote from his own perspective. But we must not push that so far that they could contradict each other. Vatican II warns us against such a thought: "Since Sacred Scripture must be read and interpreted with the same Spirit by which it was written, to rightly get the sense of the sacred texts, we must look not less diligently to the content and unity of the whole of Scripture, taking into account the living Tradition of the whole Church and the analogy of faith."[2]

Some have even dared to hint that Mark's attitude cannot fit with the virginal conception—knowing that, of course, Mary would surely believe. The result is an unspoken implication that perhaps the virginal conception was not a fact!

But, as form criticism shows,[3] Mark may have joined two once-separate scenes, in 3:21 and 31. Further, the words "his relatives," in 3-21, are quite vague in the Greek, which has *hoi par' autou*, meaning "those around him," who could be friends, relatives, members of the household. So we are not sure that Mary was in the group. And if she was, she might well have gone along to try to restrain more distant relatives who did not believe in Jesus, a thing quite normal for a mother. Even rather ordinary mothers are quite apt to stand up for a son, even when everyone else thinks him guilty.

Therefore, since as we now know, there may be two originally separate scenes in verses 21 and 31—there is not proof at all that it is the same group on the two scenes. Similarly, when Jesus speaks, in 6:4, of a prophet as without honor even among his own, He would not have to mean His mother too. It would be true enough with lesser relatives.

The fact that He asked, "Who is my mother . . .?" was merely a dramatic way of saying that of two kinds of relationships, through physical kinship and through faith, the second was the greater. Of course, Mary was greatest in both categories, as Vatican II pointed out: "In the course of her Son's preaching she received the words whereby, in extolling a kingdom beyond the calculations and bonds of flesh and blood, He declared blessed those who heard and kept the word of God, as she was faithfully doing (cf. Mk. 3:35)" (*Constitution on the Church*, n. 58).

Vatican II strongly taught Mary's total dedication to Jesus from the very start: "The Father of mercies willed that the acceptance by the planned-for-mother should precede the Incarnation, so that thus, just as a woman contributed to death, so also a woman should contribute to life. . . . And so Mary, the daughter of Adam, by consenting to the divine word, became the Mother of Jesus, and embracing the salvific will of God with full heart, held back by no sin, totally dedicated herself to the person and work of her Son, by the grace of Almighty God, serving the mystery of the redemption with Him and under Him" (n. 56).

So, clearly, she could not have failed to believe in Him as some think St. Mark said. From the very fact that He would "reign over the House of Jacob for ever," she would know that He was the Messiah, for Jews then commonly expected the Messiah to live forever. Further, as we shall see later, she had excellent reason to learn even His divinity from the message of Gabriel.

Another charge of religious error has been raised over a comparison between Isaiah 2:4 and Joel 4:10.[4] Isaiah has the familiar words: "They shall beat their swords into ploughshares and their spears into pruning hooks." But Joel pictures the Lord as saying: "Beat your ploughshares into swords, and your pruning hooks into spears."

But the critics have not done their homework. The two texts, Isaiah and Joel, speak of two different situations. Isaiah 2 is a highly poetic and idealized image of the kingdom of the Messiah. How idealized the image is, is clear from the further description in Isaiah 11:6-8: "The wolf shall dwell with the lamb, and the leopard shall lie down with the kid, and the calf and the lion and the fatling together, and a little child shall lead them. The cow and the bear shall feed; their young shall lie down together; and the lion shall eat straw like the ox. The sucking child shall play over the hole of the asp, and the weaned child shall put his hand on the adder's den."

In contrast, Joel pictures God's judgment on the nations. As a note in the New American Bible says, "Weapons are made in response to God's summons to armies which he selects to repel forever the unlawful invaders from the land of this chosen people."

Still another objection is raised from the fact that Jeremiah the prophet said that he had been deceived by God Himself (15:18; 20:7,9), and that the word of the Lord that Jeremiah had spoken had not come to pass (17:15-16).

Jeremiah really says: "Behold, they say to me, 'Where is the word of the Lord? Let it come!' I have not pressed thee to send evil, nor have I desired the day of disaster, thou knowest" (17:15-16). It is not Jeremiah who is charging that the threatened punishment has not come; it is his unbelieving countrymen. They are saying in effect: "Look, you have been threatening for some time now, but nothing happens!" But the punishment did finally come, showing that the word of the Lord was true.

Jeremiah is talking about his personal afflictions in 20:7-9. He had mistakenly thought that God had promised that he, Jeremiah, would be protected in his own person. But now Jeremiah has been scourged (20:2) and put in the stocks for the night. Jeremiah has misunderstood what God has said. It is the same with 15:18.

So the Scriptures remain true in spite of some unperceptive interpreters. There are other charges, but they too can be answered.

Chapter 9

Cardinal Koenig on Error in Scripture

An astounding thing happened at Vatican II on October 2, 1964. Cardinal Koenig of Vienna arose and charged that there were errors in matters of science and history in Scripture. Several other bishops supported him. In fact, at first, no opposition was expressed. But then a group of bishops appealed to Pope Paul VI. The final outcome was a statement in the *Constitution on Divine Revelation* (n. 11) disagreeing with Cardinal Koenig.[1]

Before stating the specific claims made by Cardinal Koenig and answering them, we need to explain the approach to Scripture by way of literary genres.

The word *genre* is taken from French (in English one sometimes meets the German *Gattung* instead). It means a literary pattern of writing. Take, for example, a modern historical novel about our Civil War. We, being natives of this culture, expect such a book to be a mixture of history and fiction. It is history in that the main line of the story is true to history and the background descriptions fit the period. We may read of steam trains and telegraphs, but not of radio, TV, or planes. On the other hand, there will be fictional fill-ins, especially word-for-word conversations between, for example, Lincoln and Grant. We expect, we even want, the author to create these fill-ins to make the story fuller and more realistic. But we do not suppose that the author really states, word for word, what these important men said. We can't even be sure that he has the substance.

The key word to notice here is *assert*. What does the writer mean to assert? He means to assert that the main line is history, that the background fits the period. But he surely does not assert that he has reported actual conversations word for word, or even their substance. So he asserts some things; other things he does not assert. The modern historical novel is a blend of history and fiction. That fact does not lead anyone to say the author is trying to deceive us or is ignorant. No, both the author and the readers know what is asserted.

This example is a specially clear one. Actually, in English we have many other genres, or literary patterns. Each of these has, as it were, rules for understanding it. Most of our genres were inherited from Greece and Rome. So long as we do our reading within that great Greek and Roman culture stream, we are able to make our adjustments of understanding—as it were, to set the dials in our head—automatically. But someone from a different culture would have to learn to make those adjustments, to learn what is or is not asserted in each genre.

Now it is obvious that Scripture belongs to a very different culture stream from ours, the ancient Semitic. Can we just assume that the ancient Semites used the same genres as we do? Of course not. That would be foolish. In fact, we would not even be faithful to Scripture if we treated it as if it had been written by a modern American. We would not be trying to find out what the ancient inspired author really meant to assert. Instead, we would be imposing our own ideas on his words. To do that is called Fundamentalism. Fundamentalists ignore genre, acting instead as if Scripture had been written by a modern American. For example, they will say that since Genesis says God made the world in six days, that means it was done in six times twenty-four hours.

Before reading any book of Scripture, we need to determine the genre being used. The genre may even vary within a biblical book. Pius XII put it this way in his great Encyclical *Divino Afflante Spiritu* (1943): "What is the literal sense in the words and writings of the ancient oriental authors is often not so obvious as with writers of our time. For what they meant to signify by their words is not determined only by the laws of grammar and philology, nor only by the context; it is altogether necessary that the interpreter mentally return, as it were, to those remote ages of the East, so that, being rightly helped by . . . history, archeology, ethnology, and other fields of knowledge, he may discern . . .

50

what literary genres . . . those writers of the ancient time wished to employ and actually employed."

Vatican II put it this way: "Since all that the inspired authors or sacred writers *assert* should be regarded as *asserted* by the Holy Spirit, we must acknowledge that the books of Scripture firmly, faithfully, and without error teach the truth which God, for the sake of our salvation, wished to be confided to Sacred Scripture" (*Constitution on Divine Revelation,* n. 11; emphases added).

This approach, through an understanding of genres, permits us to solve numerous problems that once were considered insoluble, including those raised by Cardinal Koenig. In fact, the sentence quoted above was Vatican II's answer to Cardinal Koenig. And it was to this sentence that the Council added a note referring us to earlier texts of the magisterium insisting that there is and can be no error of any kind in Scripture.

Before going ahead, let us answer a claim that is often made today. It is said that the Scripture Encyclical *Divino Afflante Spiritu* of Pope Pius XII was a real about-face, that it told Catholic scholars to use methods of a scientific approach to the Bible that had hitherto been forbidden to them, chiefly the approach by way of literary genres. (see Patrick Henry, *New Directions in New Testament Study*, Westminster, 1979, pp. 230-31.)

Was that approach really once forbidden? On June 23, 1905, the Pontifical Biblical Commission, which was supposed to be the agent of restriction, published this question and reply: "Can it be accepted as a principle of sound interpretation if we say that some books of Scripture that are considered as historical—partly or totally—do not, at times, give history strictly and objectively so called, but instead have just the appearance of history, so as to convey something other than a strict literal or historical sense of the words?" The reply was: "No, except however in the case—not easily or rashly to be admitted—in which, when the sense of the Church does not oppose it and subject to the judgment of the Church, it is proved by solid arguments that the sacred writer did not intend to hand down history strictly and properly truly so called, but, under the appearance and form of history, gave a parable, an allegory, or a sense differing from the properly literal or historical sense of the words."

The reply is carefully qualified. It deals only with writings that at first sight seem to be history, not with other genres. Can things that look like history ever be taken otherwise? They can be if there are solid proofs that the book or passage is really a different genre. We may admit that, subject to the judgment of the Church.

This is not really so different from what Pius XII said in *Divino Afflante Spiritu*: "What these [genres] are, the scholar cannot decide in advance, but only after a careful investigation of the literature of the ancient Near East." Just a few years later, in 1950, when Pius XII saw that many scholars were getting too loose, he wrote in *Humani Generis*: "We must specially deplore a certain excessively free way of interpreting the historical books of the Old Testament. . . . The first eleven chapters of Genesis, even though they do not fully match the pattern of historical composition used by the great Greek and Latin writers of history, or by modern historians, yet in a certain true sense—which needs further investigation by scholars—they do pertain to the genre of history." (How they pertain to history will be considered in chapter 11).

Further, the Biblical Commission warned that we must heed "the sense of the Church." Pius XII said the same thing in *Divino Afflante Spiritu*: "Let Scripture scholars, mindful of the fact that there is here question of a divinely inspired word whose care and interpretation is entrusted by God Himself to the Church—let them not less carefully take into account the explanations and declarations of the magisterium of the Church, and likewise the explanations given by the Holy Fathers [of the first centuries], and also the analogy of faith as Leo XIII . . . wisely noted." The expression "analogy of faith" means the entire structure of the teachings of the Church. No interpretation can clash with it, even by implication. If it does, the interpretation is false. Pius XII was somewhat more encouraging about the genre approach than was the Biblical Commission, but there was no substantial or doctrinal difference between them.

Turning to the claims of error made by Cardinal Koenig, it is good to note that floor speeches at a Council do not enjoy the providential protection promised by Christ. That protection applies only to the final statements of the Council. Actually, at the very first General Council at Nicea, in 325 A.D., several bishops denied the divinity of Christ!

The report of the speech of Cardinal Koenig says: "In Daniel 1;1 we read that King Nebuchadnezzar besieged Jerusalem in the third year of King Jehoiakim, i.e., 607 B.C., but from the authentic chronicle of King Nebuchadnezzar that has been discovered, we know that the siege can only have taken place three years later."[2] The introductory page in the Jerusalem Bible edition of the Book of Daniel notes that "the historical setting of the story undoubtedly disregards known facts, persons and dates and contains anachronisms in detail.   . . ."

The approach via literary genres, however, solves the problems easily. We must first determine the literary genre of the narrative parts of the Book of Daniel (other parts, the visions, belong to the apocalyptic genre).

It has been established by research (see Anchor Bible commentary on Daniel, pp. 46-71) that in both Jewish writing and in pagan texts there was in existence, by the time of the Book of Daniel, a genre called "the edifying narrative." The story might or might not have a basis in fact. Even if it did, it was handled very freely. Its relationship to strict hagiography would be much like the relationship of science fiction to science. The original readers recognized it for what it was, yet they found that it gave them a sort of spiritual lift. It is to this genre that the narrative parts of Daniel belong. It is idle, therefore, to charge them with historical error. The author simply did not mean to *assert* that he was writing history. He was not. He was writing a different genre, the edifying narrative. So the "problem" Cardinal Koenig thought insoluble turns out to be no problem at all.

Cardinal Koenig gave two other alleged instances of errors in Scripture. Although these "errors" do not need the genre approach for solution, it is convenient to look at them here.

According to Mark 2:26, David entered the house of God under the high priest Abiathar, said Cardinal Koenig. But really, according to 1 Samuel 21:1ff., it was not under Abiathar but under his father, Ahimelech.

The answer is easily found with the help of Greek grammar. The Greek text here has *epi Abiathar archiereos.* Now Greek *epi* followed by a genitive of the person can readily have a generic time meaning, i.e., "in the days of," according to a standard reference work, *Greek Grammar for Colleges,* by H. W. Smyth, par. 1689. Smyth gives as an example, Thucydides 7:86, *ep'emou,* meaning "in my time." So the expression in Mark 2:26 really means "in the time of Abiathar" and not necessarily "when Abiathar was high priest." Abiathar's name was chosen to designate the period because he was better known to readers of the Old Testament than his father, Ahimelech, and because Abiathar was closely associated with King David.

In Matthew 27:9, we read that in the fate of Judas, a prophecy of

Jeremiah was fulfilled. But, objected Cardinal Koenig, it was really Zechariah 11:12f. that was quoted.

Again, the answer is easy. A note in the not excessively conservative New American Bible on the passage in question, says that "Matthew's free citation of Jer. 18,2f; 19,1f; 32,6-15 and Zec. 11,13 shows that he regards Judas' death as a divine judgment." Matthew was putting together passages from Jeremiah and Zechariah, chiefly Jeremiah 32:6-15 and Zechariah 11:13. As to the fact that Matthew puts the name Jeremiah on the combined text, it was a rabbinic practice to use the name of the best-known author in such combined texts.

Chapter 10

Pope Leo XIII on Principles of History

Some confusion arose from a remark of Leo XIII about the genre of history. One might wish that he had spoken more fully and clearly. However, we can, by careful study, find out what he did mean.

In his great Scripture Encyclical *Providentissimus Deus* (1893), this Pope observed that the inspired writers sometimes wrote according to appearance in matters of science. Even today we also speak the same way, when for example, we say the sun rises or sets, or moves through the sky. Pope Leo says this in paragraph 121 in *Enchiridion Biblicum* (Arnodo, Romae, 1954). Then in paragraph 122 he notes that while we must defend the truth of Scripture, this does not mean that we have to accept every proposal of individual Fathers of the Church, or of interpreters. They may have been affected by the view of their times about matters of science. He says that we must also distinguish various philosophical notions, which may be in the minds of these writers, from the solid truth of Scripture. Notions in both science and philosophy come and go. Things held as true today may be rejected tomorrow.

Right after these remarks, Pope Leo says that "it will help to transfer these things to other fields of knowledge, especially to history." In the very next sentence, he adds that some have excessive confidence in ancient pagan records and are inclined to believe the pagan records instead of Scripture when the two seem to clash.

What the Pope had in mind in suggesting we "transfer these things . . . to history" is not as clear as we would like. As a result, Pope Benedict XV, in his Scripture Encyclical *Spiritus Paraclitus* (1920), felt the need to guard against a possible false interpretation of the words of Pope Leo. "Why should we refute at length," wrote Benedict, "a thing clearly injurious to our Predecessor, and false, and full of error? For what parallel is there between natural phenomena and history? Natural things deal with what appears to the senses . . . but the chief law of history, on the contrary, is that the writings should really fit with what really happened. If we say that we could use a relative truth in historical matters in Scripture, how will that truth stand about the complete immunity from error which our Predecessor insisted on in Scripture?" So what Pope Leo says about history, did not apply "across the board" (Latin *universe*).

It is not surprising that those who are quite ready to charge errors of all kinds in Scripture itself should also be ready to charge error to Pope Leo XIII. After saying that the inspired writers could write about natural phenomena according to appearances, Pope Leo XIII seemed to add, as we saw above, that the same principles applied to history as to the natural sciences. The charge is therefore that Leo meant that history could be written not according to facts, but according to appearances. Therefore, the objectors continue, Benedict XV felt the need to correct the error of Leo XIII in his *Spiritus Paraclitus* of 1920.[1]

But Leo XIII rejected every kind of error in Scripture. Nor did he admit error by the backdoor, as it were, in saying Scripture may speak of scientific matters according to common appearances. But when we consider the Pope's remark in the framework of what we now know about genre, we see he was saying that the sacred writers did not *assert* that such things were accurate scientific knowledge. Further, Pope Leo insisted, as did Pope Benedict XV, on complete freedom from error in Scripture.

But there are two other things Pope Leo clearly meant, as is clear when we consider his words in context.

First, Pope Leo said in paragraph 122 that we need not accept every theory of science or philosophy; and in paragraph 123 he said that we need not accept every pagan record in preference to Scripture. Actually, we know that many ancient kings did a lot of boasting in their records. In Egypt, some were even known to use victory monuments of earlier times, substituting their own names for the names of the earlier kings.

Second, as Pope Benedict XV keenly observed, the remark of Leo XIII about applying similar principles to history and natural science—talking according to common appearances and usual ways of speaking—must not be taken across the board *(universe)* as if applying to every case. This implies two things: that there are cases in which seemingly historical things deal only in popularly expressed appearances; and that there are cases in which we must say instead that history does record facts as they really were.

We can find examples of each kind. Thus our Lord Himself and St. Paul, too, commonly spoke of King David as the author of *all* the psalms. They were following the usual way of speaking. St. Paul may not have known that all the psalms were not by David, but Jesus surely knew the truth. Yet it was quite right for both to speak according to what was the usual appearance of the case. To use our language of genre, they did not mean to *assert* that such was the strict truth about authorship.

Similarly, our Lord could compare Himself to Jonah. As we shall see, there is a large question about the historicity of Jonah. But Jesus did not intend to reveal that matter—it did not pertain at all to His purpose—and so He did not *assert* that Jonah was historical. He merely made use of common beliefs to illustrate a point. One of us could quote a line from *Alice in Wonderland* to illustrate something without believing that charming fancy was historical.

Again, in John 8:33, some Jews tell Jesus that they are descendants of Abraham. Perhaps they really were. But many scholars today, considering the genre of Exodus to be something like epic, think that many elements of diverse origin were welded together into a people by Exodus and Sinai. Then not all would spring from Abraham. Exodus 12:38 says that when Israel left Egypt, "a mixed multitude also went up with them." Again, the same situation (see also Numbers 11:4). By the time of Jesus, many had joined Judaism as proselytes. In spite of this, Jesus accepts the usual way of speaking and does not challenge their claim to be descendants of Abraham.

Did the inspired author of the Book of Jonah mean to write history or, instead, an extended parable to teach some important things? There is no doubt that the book, whether or not it is historical, does teach some important points. But with the present state of the evidence, and since the Church has given no decision, the answer must remain uncertain.

There is no great difficulty about the great fish that swallowed Jonah. God could, by a miracle, have brought that about. In fact, some think He could have done it without much of a miracle, except for having the fish at the right place at the right time, and for having the fish disgorge Jonah at the right time and place. Wallechninsky and Wallace[2] tell us that in February 1891, after the ship *Star of the East* had caught an eighty-foot sperm whale, a seaman, James Bartley, was missing. After a search, he was presumed drowned. But the next day, when the crew was cutting up the fish, Bartley was found alive inside the whale.

But much of the problem centers on the things said concerning the city of Nineveh. Jonah 3:3 says that Nineveh *was* a large city. Some think that this word implies that Nineveh had fallen by the time the book was written (it fell in 612 B.C.). If we think, as some do, that Jonah wrote the book and that he belongs in the reign of Jeroboam II, King of Israel (perhaps 793-753), we have a problem. (Second Kings 14:25 speaks of Jonah ben Amittai, the prophet, as being alive then.) But there is no need to hold that Jonah himself wrote the book. He might have had the experiences; another hand could have written them down later. The *was* on the other hand, could be just part of the vocabulary of storytelling.

More serious is the statement of Jonah 3:3: "Now Nineveh was an exceedingly great city, three days' journey in breadth." The ruins of Nineveh which have been found, do not show a city nearly that large. A. Parrot[3] suggests that the name Nineveh could have referred to a twenty-six-mile string of settlements in the Assyrian triangle. Another view is that Jonah would likely speak at the city gates, where people gathered to converse. As there were many such gates to Nineveh, it would take three days to spend some time talking at each.

Again, in Jonah 4:11, God says that in Nineveh "there are more than a hundred and twenty thousand people who do not know their right hand from their left." It is argued that the hundred and twenty thousand must have been babies, since they could not tell right from left. The objectors add that Deuteronomy 1:39 and Isaiah 7:15-16 use that expression to mean babies. That many babies would suppose a huge populace. A check of those two passages shows that the language is not the same; they speak of those who cannot know good from bad, or of learning to reject bad and choose good. The expression in Jonah then could mean that in the matter of religion the people of Nineveh simply do not know the ABCs.

Jonah 3:6 speaks of "the king of Nineveh." That was not the usual expression among the Assyrians. The king was called king of Ashur. On the other hand, Jonah need not have adopted the expression of the Assyrians.

Some object that the Hebrew text of Jonah shows some words that were not in the language at the time of Jonah himself, for example, *ta' am* (3:7), to mean "mandate." There is also the late expression "God of Heaven" in 1:9. But this objection cannot prove anything because, as has already been noted, the Jews sometimes deliberately updated the language of their ancient texts to make them more readily intelligible.

A more serious objection is that at the time of Jeroboam II, when Jonah lived, Nineveh was not the residence of the king of Assyria. Nineveh became the capital much later, under Sennacherib (704-681). The only possible reply would be to suppose—a thing for which we lack evidence—that there was a lesser ruler in Nineveh who might be referred to as king. This is not really likely. Further, the omission of any statement of time could point to a parable rather than to history. The mention of Jonah by Jesus, as we saw above, is inconclusive. He could merely have been making a literary allusion.

In all, then, the evidence against making the historicity of the Book of Jonah is not fully conclusive, though the problem of when Nineveh became the king's residence is a very difficult one.

On the other hand, quite independently of the question of genre, it is easy to see that the chief purpose of the book was to teach two very important lessons, which are more important in themselves than the question of history.

First, in the minds of the Jews and other nearby peoples, the Assyrians were the world's worse people. They went in for calculated terrorism in war. When they finally captured a city, they would cruelly kill many of the leading men to try to scare others out of resisting them. The Book of Jonah, nonetheless, shows God as concerned about the well-being of even the Assyrians (to love is to will or wish good to others for their sake). Now if God can love even the Assyrians, He must love everybody. This is a most important truth taught by the Book of Jonah.

The second truth, though hardly noticed by scholars, is of great importance. Prophets who were sent to the chosen People of God, the

Hebrews, invariably received harsh treatment if not death. But when a prophet comes to someone outside the People of God, even to the Assyrians, he is welcomed.

This point has a tremendous implication. Membership, full membership, in the People of God is a great privilege, very helpful for eternal salvation. Yet we know that salvation can be had even without it, though less safely. Thus Pius IX, in *Quanto Conficiamur Moerore* (August 10, 1863),[4] said, "God, in his supreme goodness and clemency, by no means allows anyone to be punished with eternal punishments who does not have the guilt of voluntary fault."

One who keeps the moral law as he knows it, therefore will be saved. He needs a certain minimum faith, yes. But Pius IX indicates that in some way—he does not say how—that faith will be present if only the person keeps the moral law. Many primitives and pagans do that, as anthropology today shows. Similarly, Vatican II taught: "They who with no fault of their own do not know the Gospel of Christ and His Church, but yet seek God with a sincere heart, and carry out His will, known through conscience, under the influence of grace, can attain eternal salvation" (*Constitution on the Church*, n. 16).

Given human frailty and the fact that it takes time for the Gospel to reach everywhere, it is inevitable that some will live their lives in a situation where it is unlikely they will attain full membership in the People of God, the Church. (We speak of "full membership," since it seems that those pagans referred to by Pius IX, Pius XII, and Vatican II must have some degree of membership.)

Hence there is a decision to be made by Divine Providence: how to assign people of all times and ages to positions in time and place where they will or will not be apt to attain that full membership. God, like a good Father, would seem to give more help to those who need more. In a normal family, a sickly child gets added attention. So God probably gives extra help where it is needed.

In other words, those who are relatively more resistant to grace need more, so they get more; that is, God arranges things so that they get full membership with its added helps. Those who are less resistant can be saved with fewer external helps—Protestants who have only a few sacraments, or even pagans, who have no sacraments. (Perhaps, too, those who are so terribly resistant as to be lost no matter what position in time and place is assigned to them may be given the least positions, so as to decrease their responsibility, and to leave the best places open to those who will profit by them.)[5]

The idea that God acts this way seems to be implied also in Ezekiel 3:5-7, Luke 17:11-19, and in the parable of the Good Samaritan. So the Book of Jonah has two powerful lessons to teach. These are its chief purpose, rather than the assertion of the historicity of the narrative or the telling of stories as vehicles for teaching.

Incidentally, the lack of any historical evidence for a conversion of Nineveh to Judaism by Jonah is a point against deciding this book to be in the historical genre.

Any Catholic reader who is not insulted by the second teaching we have seen in Jonah has not understood our reasoning!

Chapter 11

Genre of Genesis

We feel great need of the genre approach when we read Genesis, chapters 1-3. We already saw that Pius XII deplored excessive looseness in the application of genres to Genesis. He insisted that the first eleven chapters of Genesis, "even though they do not fully match the pattern of historical composition used by the great Greek and Latin writers of history, or by modern historians, yet in a certain sense—which needs further investigation by scholars—they do pertain to the genre of history."

So let us try to carry out the desire of Pius XII. Those chapters of Genesis pertain to history in that they do relate events that really happened. They present the facts within the special framework of a story, however. We might even call it a stage setting. Hence Genesis 1-11 is historical in that it tells what really happened, chiefly these: God made all things; in some special way, He made the first human pair; He gave them some command (we do not know what the command was—the garden and the fruit are part of the stage setting); they violated the command and fell from favor.

GOD MADE MAN IN SOME SPECIAL WAY. St. Augustine, in his commentary on Genesis (*De Genesi ad litterams* 6.12.20), rejected a simplistic interpretation of these Scriptures: "That God made man with bodily hands from the clay," wrote Augustine, "is an excessively childish thought . . ., we should rather believe the one who wrote it used a metaphorical term, instead of supposing God is bounded by such lines of limbs as we see in our bodies."

In this same vein, Pius XII wrote: "The Magisterium of the Church does not forbid that the theory of evolution about the origin of the human body as coming from pre-existing and living matter be investigated and discussed by experts in both fields, so far as the present state of human sciences and sacred theology permits—for Catholic faith requires us to hold that the human soul is immediately created by God. This is to be done in such a way that the reasons on both sides, for and against, be weighed and judged with due gravity, moderation and temperance, provided all are prepared to submit to the judgment of the Church. . . . They go too far in rash daring who act as if the origin of the human body from pre-existent and living matter were already fully proved by evidence discovered up to now and by reasoning on that evidence, as if there were nothing in the sources of divine revelation calling for very great moderation and caution" (*Humani Generis*).[1]

In summary, then, we are permitted to study evolution scientifically and with theological care, but we must not say that the evidence is such that the theory is fully proved at present.

That caution was written in 1950. Has scientific evidence developed to the point that evolution has now been proved?

The "Research News" section in *Science* magazine for November 21, 1980, gives a long report on what *Science* calls "a historic conference in Chicago [that] challenges the four-decade-long dominance of the Modern Synthesis." The Modern Synthesis is the belief that "Evolution . . . moves at a stately pace, with small changes accumulating over periods of many millions of years." The report tells us that "a wide spectrum of researchers—ranging from geologists and paleontologists, through ecologists and population geneticists to embryologists and molecular biologists—gathered in Chicago's Field Museum of Natural History" to consider evolution.

The Modern Synthesis came under heavy challenge, for: "The problem is that according to most paleontologists the principle [sic] feature of individual species within the fossil record is stasis, not change. . . . For the most part, the fossils do not document a smooth transition from old morphologies to new ones. 'For millions of years species remain unchanged in the fossil record,' said Stephen Jay Gould of Harvard, 'and they then abruptly disappear, to be replaced by something that is substantially different but clearly related.'"

The result is a shift. The evidence that was supposed to support evolution—gradual changes in the fossil record, of one species into another—has been found almost entirely lacking. So, do the scientists drop the theory of evolution once they find that the evidence is not sufficient to prove it? No, they make an adjustment in the theory instead: "The emerging picture of evolutionary change . . . is one of periods during which individual species remain virtually unchanged, punctuated by abrupt events at which a descendant species arises from the original stock." In other words, there has been a whole series of flukes, sudden leaps from lower to higher. What is the proof of this? If there was anyone at the conference who knew, that person failed to speak up.

Newsweek (November 3, 1980, pp. 95-96) summed up the same meeting this way: "In the fossil record, missing links are the rule. . . . Evidence from fossils now points overwhelmingly away from the classical Darwinism which . . . [says] that new species evolve out of existing ones by the gradual accumulation of small changes. . . . Increasingly, scientists now believe that species change little for millions of years, and then evolve quickly, in a kind of quantum leap—not necessarily in a direction that represents an obvious improvement in fitness. The majority of 160 of the world's top paleontologists, anatomists, evolutionary geneticists and developmental biologists supported some form of this theory of 'punctuated equilibria.'"

Pius XII is still right: there is no proof. But we may discuss evolution as long as we admit this fact, and as long as we do not make the theory atheistic. Sadly, there seems to be a tendency of this kind in many scientists. Thus, according to the article in *Science*, at one point Niles Eldredge of the American Museum of Natural History, New York, found himself "countering accusations of monotheism." Really, to suppose that beings can lift themselves by their bootstraps, adding higher perfections that they receive from nowhere, is untenable on the grounds of reason alone, even without the help of religion.

Closely related is the question of polygenism, the theory that our race descended not from one pair but from several. The task of proving this scientifically is awesome, probably impossible. One would have to find the oldest human remains and be sure they were human. Where there is evidence of ritual burial, especially with artifacts, one may be sure that the remains are clearly human. Otherwise it is often impossible to know. Scientists still differ over the recent fossil skeleton of "Lucy." But to prove polygenism, one would have to be certain that the remains are human and, further, that they are close to the origin of the race that, considering geographic distribution, they could not have come from one pair.

We are still countless miles from having such proof. In fact, *Science News* (August 13, 1983, p. 101) reports that Allan Wilson of the University of California at Berkley now holds that "we all go back to one mother, living 350,000 years ago. . . . Wilson found 110 variations in the mitochondrial DNA of 112 individuals in a world-wide survey." (Mitochondria are the power-producing structures of cells. They contain 35 genes that are passed directly from mother to child, hence Wilson did not speak of a father.)

From the viewpoint of Scripture, Pius XII said, in *Humani Generis:* "Christians cannot embrace that opinion . . . since it is by no means apparent how this view could be reconciled with things which the sources of revelations and the *acta* of the Magisterium of the Church teach about original sin, which comes from a sin really committed by one Adam, and which, being transmitted by generation, is in each one as his own."

Of the scholars who sincerely wish to follow the Church, some think that this statement completely rules out polygenism; others, who also seek to be loyal, think that its careful wording leaves a door open by saying that polygenism cannot be accepted because it is not clear how to fit it with Scripture and official teaching. They think that if a way could be found to make it fit, the objection brought by Pius XII would be dropped.

A special problem with these chapters of Genesis is the account of how Eve was made from a rib of Adam. Pope John Paul II explained excellently in his audience of November 7, 1979,[2] that Genesis 1-3 is "myth." Scripture scholars often describe the genre of Genesis 1-3 in that way, but they do not mean what most people think of on hearing the word *myth*. As the Pope explained, "the term *myth* does not designate a fabulous content, but merely an archaic way of expressing a deeper content."[3]

Within this framework, the Pope then explained the rib scene: "The man (Adam) falls into the 'sleep' in order to wake up 'male' and 'female'. . . . Perhaps . . . the analogy of sleep indicates here not so much a passing from consciousness to subconsciousness as a specific return to non-being (sleep contains an element of annihilation of man's conscious existence), that is, to the moment preceding the creation, in order that, through God's creative initiative, solitary 'man' may

66

emerge from it again in his double unity as male and female.   .   . It is a question here of homogeneity of the whole being of both."[4] The Pope adds: "It is interesting to note that for the ancient Sumerians the cuneiform sign to indicate the noun *rib* coincided with the one used to indicate the word *life*."[5]

St. John Chrysostom, centuries ago, in his *Homily on Genesis* (2:21), moved in the same direction as the Pope, without being able to work it out fully. He called the rib episode a case of *synkatabasis*, divine adaptation to our needs. "See the condescendence of divine Scripture," says Chrysostom, "what words it uses because of our weakness. 'And He took,' it says, 'one of his ribs.' Do not take what is said in a human way, but understand that the crassness of the words fits human weakness."

If we work within this same framework of genre, we can find other remarkable insights into the content. Let us retell the episode in our own words so as to bring out these points.

Eve is in the garden one day. Along comes the tempter and says: "This is a fine garden! Do they let you eat the fruit of all these trees?" Eve replies: "Yes .   . oh, pardon me, not the one over there. God said if we eat from that one, we will die." The evil one responds: "He said that? Can't you see He is selfish, holding out on you? Why, if you eat that fruit, you will become like gods. He does not want anyone else to get what He has." So Eve looks at the fruit and says, "I can just *see* that it is good."

Eve's words imply: *God may know what is good in some things, but here I can see for myself. This is good, even if He says it is not.*

Here the ancient theologian of Genesis was telling us that every sin is, at bottom, pride. God may know some things, but I know better here and now. My senses tell me for certain what is good.

After Adam and Eve sinned, God calls: "Adam, where are you?" Adam says, "I hid myself because I was naked." Then God asks Adam, "How did you find out you were naked if you did not eat the forbidden fruit?"

Adam and Eve were naked both before and after the first sin. But before sinning, that fact did not disturb them. Afterwards, feeling ashamed, they hurriedly improvised some covering from leaves. What seems to be implied is this: Man, if God had given him only the essentials of humanity, no added gifts, would have had to work to control his drives. Man has many drives in his body, each legitimate in itself, each working towards its own satisfaction. Each operates automatically, blindly, taking no thought for the well-being of the whole man. So, there would be need for mortification to learn to tame them. The sex drive, especially, is unruly. It can start up without a man wanting it to start.

But, clearly, before the Fall, Adam had no such problem. His sex drive was not rebellious. It could operate, but only when he told it to, not before. But after the Fall, that drive began to take over, to operate without his willing it. Hence the feeling of need for cover.

Before the Fall, Adam had had what we might call a coordinating gift, a power that made it easy to keep all his drives harmonious and in subjection to his reason and will. After the Fall, he lost that coordinating gift. And, inasmuch as feelings, especially strong ones, can pull on one's judgment, the result of sin was that the mind was darkened and the will weakened. We, descendants of Adam, did not inherit the special gift. Adam and Eve had thrown it away by sin; they no longer had it to give.

Having lost God's favor, His grace, their descendants could not inherit it. To be born without grace in the soul is to be in a state of sin. In the infant, that state is not the child's own fault; in the adult sinner, that person is culpable. To lose God's favor means that what is said in John 14:23 cannot come true: "If a man loves me, he will keep my word, and my Father will love him, and we will come to him and make our home with him." In theological language, this means that the soul will lack the divine presence it had in sanctifying grace. Adam and Eve lost this favor, and so this grace. Their descendants were born without it. They begin their earthly lives without the divine presence within their souls that is the uncreated aspect of sanctifying grace. That is what is meant by original sin.

St. Paul, under inspiration, in Romans 5:12, saw this in Genesis, and the Council of Trent authoritatively interpreted it thus.[6]

(Of course this does not preclude the fact that Adam, Eve, and their descendants could, after the unfortunate start, regain that favor and grace.)

Chapter 12

Genre of Infancy Gospels

What is the genre of the Infancy Gospels (chapters 1 and 2 of Matthew and Luke)? Many scholars in recent times have been inclined to say that it is midrash, a rather loose Hebrew genre which investigates hidden meanings and attempts to apply them to new situations. If the Infancy Gospels are midrash, many things in the narratives—the star, the Magi—may not really be historical.[1]

R. E. Brown (*The Birth of the Messiah*, Doubleday, 1977) seems to think that no one has fully identified the genre of the Infancy Gospels. He speaks of these chapters as theological introductions built on few facts. Luke, Brown thinks, built up a few scant bits of information by making his account parallel to Old Testament incidents (pp. 37-38, 557-562).

Brown sees evidence of unhistorical character in several things. In the Gospel of St. Matthew (2:11), unlike that of Luke, Brown notes that "Mary and Joseph live in Bethlehem of Judea, and have their home there" (p. 124). "Matthew," writes Brown, "does not tell us precisely where in Bethlehem Jesus was born, but verse 11 [of chapter 2 of Matthew] suggests the birthplace was the house where Mary (and Joseph) lived. The Lucan version . . . wherein Mary and Joseph were visitors to Bethlehem without a place to stay . . . led to the subsequent Christian tradition that Jesus was born in a cave" (p. 166).

Brown also thinks that the census mentioned by St. Luke could not be historical (pp. 547-555). He says that "a journey to Egypt is quite irreconcilable with Luke's account of an orderly and uneventful return from Bethlehem to Nazareth shortly after the birth of the child" (p. 225). Brown also notes that "the angel speaks to Joseph in Matthew, while he speaks to Mary in Luke" (p. 35).

Brown's objections are very easily answered. In Matthew 2:11, we find the wise men "going into the house [where] they saw the child with Mary his mother." Mary and Joseph did come to Bethlehem for the registration. Not finding a suitable place for the birth of the child, they took refuge in a cave. But the Magi need not have arrived at once. The fact that Herod ordered a slaughter of children two years of age and under suggests there was some lapse of time. In that interval came the Presentation in the Temple and a return to Bethlehem. Although they did not intend to settle there permanently, Joseph would obviously have found a house there instead of going back to the cave. It was in that house that the Magi found them.

The Greek *apographe* is broader than the English *census*. It could mean a different kind of enrollment. A new study, *The Birth of Christ Recalculated* (E. L. Martin, 2nd ed. FBR Publications, Pasadena, 1980), concludes that it really was a registration to profess allegiance to Augustus, in preparation for his receiving the great title *Pater Patriae* ("Father of His Country") in 2 B.C. A restudy of astronomical data and of an old inscription, the Lapis Tiburtinus, leads to the conclusion that Mary and Joseph went to Bethlehem in September of 3 B.C., probably on September 11. Martin's work, which has received good reviews, readily solves the problems of the census. It, incidentally, also solves a number of previously unsolvable problems of the secular history of the time. (The ancient historian Josephus, in his *Antiquities*, places the death of Herod just after a lunar eclipse. But there had been several in the years we are concerned with.)

The journey to Egypt presents no problem either. Luke 2:39 is just a summary account with no indication at all of time. Scholars in other places (for example, in *The Jerome Biblical Commentary* II, p. 229, on the problem of the relation of the Council of Jerusalem to statements by St. Paul) are quite willing to consider the possibility that Luke had telescoped two council meetings into one account.

Finally, Brown's worry over the fact that, in Matthew, the angel speaks to Joseph, while in Luke, he speaks to Mary is surprisingly inane. In Luke, the angel first brought the message to Mary, asking her consent. She, in humility, told no one, not even Joseph. So an angel had to be sent later to inform him.

70

On the contrary, there are strong reasons for believing in the factual character of the Infancy Gospels. St. Luke in his opening verses tells us that "many others have undertaken to draw up accounts" about Jesus. It is clear that Luke has consulted these other accounts and intends to be very careful. Would Luke, right after such a declaration of intent, immediately turn to so highly fanciful a genre as Brown thinks he does? John L. McKenzie, in general a friend of Brown's, in his review of *The Birth of the Messiah*, said: "One wonders how a gentile convert (or a gentile proselyte) could have acquired so quickly the mastery of the Greek Old Testament shown in the use of the Old Testament in Luke's infancy narratives. If Luke the physician had been able to study medicine with such success, he would have discovered a cure for cancer. . . . Luke must have had a source for his Old Testament texts and allusions; and as it is hard to think of such a collection of texts without a narrative for them to illustrate, a pre-Lucan infancy narrative is suggested, I beg to submit."[2]

Further evidence of Luke's great care for accuracy appears in an article, "Did St. Luke imitate the Septuagint?"[3] Luke's Greek shows more Semitic influence (Hebrew or Aramaic) than does the Greek of those New Testament writers who really were Semites. The strongest instance is in his use of apodotic *kai*, that is, inserting *and* to start the main clause. For example, Luke 5:1 says, "And it happened when the crowd pressed on Him to hear the word of God, *and* He stood by the Lake of Gennesaret." (Emphasis added. My translation—standard versions avoid reproducing Semitisms.) The word *and* is out of place in English. It was also out of place in normal Greek, and even in normal Aramaic. But Hebrew in the Old Testament commonly used it in certain situations (apodotic *wau* = *and*). Now the usual view has been that Luke resorted to such Semitisms to give his writing biblical flavor by imitating the Greek of the Septuagint (the old version of the Old Testament). It would be much as if we were to inject *thee, thou*, etc., to lend our own writing a biblical flavor. But a statistical study shows Luke was not imitating the Septuagint, for an actual count of examples of apodotic *kai* in Luke shows that he used it only twenty to twenty-five percent of the times where he would have if he had been imitating the Septuagint, which almost always reproduces it when the Hebrew has the apodotic *wau*. Imagine the absurdity of someone today trying to give his work a biblical flavor by using *thee* and *thou*, but using such expressions only about a quarter of the time! So Luke had a different reason. If we believe his claim to have used sources, he could have found documents in Hebrew, Aramaic, and Greek. Since Aramaic does not normally have the apodotic *wau*, the source of Luke's structure must be that he used Hebrew documents and translated them with extreme, really excessive care. The same phenomenon appears in some old Latin versions of Scripture made from Greek. These translations import Greek structures into Latin, and we know that this was done out of concern for complete accuracy. So Luke did use documents, used them with extreme care.

Vatican II, in its *Constitution on Divine Revelation*, taught: "Holy Mother the Church firmly and most constantly has held and does hold that the four Gospels we mentioned, whose historicity it unhesitatingly affirms, faithfully hand down what Jesus the Son of God, living among men, really did and taught for their eternal salvation. . . . The sacred authors wrote the four Gospels, selecting certain things out of many things handed down orally or in writing, making a synthesis of certain things, or explaining them with attention to the state of the churches, and retaining the form of proclamation, in such a way always that they communicated true and sincere things about Jesus to us" (n. 19). This statement of Vatican II makes no exception for the Infancy Gospels, thus they too are to be considered historical.[4]

Vatican II's *Constitution on the Church,* following up on this statement, treats events of the Infancy Gospels as fully factual: "This union of the Mother with the Son in the work of salvation is evident from the time of the virginal conception of Christ even to His death. In the first place, it is evident when Mary, arising in haste to visit Elizabeth, is greeted by her as blessed because of her faith . . . [it is evident] at His birth, when the Mother of God joyfully showed her firstborn Son—who did not diminish, but consecrated her virginal integrity—to the shepherds and the Magi" (n. 57). Note how unqualifiedly Vatican II speaks of even the shepherds and the Magi, though shortly before in paragraph 55, it had very carefully hedged its language by writing, "*cf.* Gen. 3:15 and *cf.* Is. 7:14," to avoid saying flatly that the human authors understood the words as Messianic, even though the Church "in the light of later and full revelation" sees more (n. 55).

In paragraph 56, Vatican II goes into much detail, and with great care, on the Annunciation: "The Father of mercies willed that the acceptance by the planned-for Mother should precede the Incarnation, so that thus, just as a woman contributed to death, so also a woman should contribute to life. Being adorned with the splendors of altogether singular holiness from the first instant of her conception, the Virgin of Naza-reth, by command of God, is hailed by the angel of the Annunciation as 'full of grace' (cf. Lk. 1:28), and she responds to the heavenly messen-ger: 'I am the handmaid of the Lord, let it be done to me according to your word' (Lk. 1:38). And so Mary, the daughter of Adam, by consent-ing to the divine word, became the Mother of Jesus, and embracing the salvific will of God with full heart, held back by no sin, totally dedicated herself as the handmaid of the Lord to the person and work of her Son."

The special precision employed by the Council appears again in the fact that it used *cf.* with Luke 1:28 but not with 1:38. In the former, the Council did, as we just saw, use the words "full of grace" for Luke 1:28, as it is in the Vulgate translation. The *cf.* seems to mean the Council did not wish to guarantee that translation—which is defensible yet debatable—while definitely making its own the thought that she was full of grace, whether that conclusion be derived from Luke 1:28 or from other sources. In contrast, there is no *cf.* with Luke 1:38, which the Council accepts as fully true. Plainly, the Council treats the scene as fully historical, even in detail.

Pope Paul VI spoke strongly on the historicity of the Infancy Gospels (allocution of December 28, 1966, *Insegnamenti di Paolo VI*, IV, pp. 678-679, Vatican Press, 1966). He complained that some "try to diminish the historical value of the Gospels themselves, especially those that refer to the birth of Jesus and His infancy. We mention this devalu-ation briefly so that you may know how to defend with study and faith the consoling certainty that these pages are not inventions of people's fancy, but that they speak the truth. 'The Apostles,' writes one who understands these things, Cardinal Bea, 'had a true historical interest. We do not mean a historical interest in the sense of Greek and Roman historiography, that is, of a logically and chronologically arranged ac-count that is an end in itself, but a concern with past events as such and an intention to report and faithfully hand down things done and said in the past.' A confirmation of this is the very concept of 'witness,' 'testi-mony,' 'testify,' which in varied forms appears more than 150 times in the New Testament. The authority of the Council has not pronounced differently on this: 'The Sacred Authors wrote . . . always in such a way that they reported on Jesus with sincerity and truth' (*Constitution on Divine Revelation*, n. 19)."

Nor is there any problem of accepting the account of Matthew 2:4-6 that King Herod could ask the Jewish scholars where Christ was to be born and get the correct answer. Micah 5:1-3 is entirely clear on that point. Further, there are Targums, ancient Jewish Aramaic translations plus commentary on the Old Testament. The date of these is debated. A reasonable conjecture in general would place them within a century before or after Christ. Regardless of the date, they are ancient and do show what the Jews could understand of the prophecies without the benefit of the hindsight of seeing them fulfilled in Christ, whom they did not accept. Samson H. Levey has gathered numerous texts recognized by the Jews as Messianic (*The Messiah: An Aramaic Interpretation*, Hebrew Union College, Cincinnati, 1974). Among others is Genesis 49:10: "The scepter shall not pass from Judah, nor the mace from between his feet, until he comes to whom it belongs" (Jerusalem Bible). The Targum Neofiti is clearer: "Kings shall not be lacking from the house of Judah . . . until the time at which King Messiah will come." Yes, there were Babylonian and Persian overlords earlier, but there was at least some kind of ruler from Judah up to Herod, in whose time Jesus was born.

The Virgin Mary, who of course would know these too, understood more fully, being full of grace. The words of the angel that her Son would "rule over the house of Jacob forever" would tell any Jew that the Son was the Messiah, for the Messiah was expected to live forever. When we add that He would be conceived by the overshadowing of the Holy Spirit—language reminiscent of the words used to describe the Divine Presence filling the ancient tabernacle in the desert (Exodus 40:34-35)—and that "for this reason" (Greek *dio*, in Luke 1:35) He would be called "Son of God," it was not hard to see that the Son was not called that in the way any Jew could be so called, but in a strictly unique sense: the son produced by the Divine Presence.

Finally, we need not labor to reconcile the genealogies in Matthew and Luke. We know today that genealogies were a special genre in ancient times, and did not necessarily give actual physical descent. They could stand for other things.[5] Artificiality is evident in the genealogy in Matthew. Verse 1:17 tells us we have sets of fourteen generations each in his list. The reason: the Hebrews used the alphabetic characters for numbers also. The word *David* could be read as *fourteen*.

Chapter 13

The Apocalyptic Books

Did ancient astronauts from another planet visit the Hebrews in Old Testament times? Arriving in "chariots of the gods," did they enjoy deluding the earthlings into thinking that they were gods? Is this the origin of the marvels in the Old Testament? Some today are foolish enough to believe such things.

In Daniel, we read this description of what he saw: "As I looked, thrones were placed and one that was ancient of days took his seat; his raiment was white as snow, and the hair of his head like pure wool; his throne was fiery flames, its wheels were burning fire. A stream of fire issued and came forth from before him; a thousand thousands served him, and ten thousand times ten thousand stood before him; the court sat in judgment, and the books were opened" (7:9-10).

"See," say some misguided moderns, "there you have a description of a spaceship. The stream of fire was the rocket exhaust."

Yet, the answer is very simple. We must investigate the literary genre of such scriptural passages. In Daniel there are two genres. One, the edifying narrative, was discussed in chapter 9. All Scripture scholars agree that the visions, such as the one just quoted, are examples of a very bizarre genre called apocalyptic.

The apocalyptic genre is special to the ancient Jews. Its fully developed form first appears in the second century B.C and had a run of about four centuries. The chief characteristics of the genre are these: (1) authorship is anonymous, or the author is given a fictitious name; (2) the genre tells of dreams and visions; (3) it includes prophecies, often made *after* the event; (4) it employs colorful, even extremely bizarre imagery; (5) it professes to contain esoteric things, secrets not known by most people.

Apocalyptic genre was first developed for the purpose of consolation in time of great stress. The Book of Daniel was intended as a consolation to console the Jews during the persecution of Antiochus IV Epiphanes of Syria (reigned 175-164 B.C.). Antiochus tried to get the Jews to abandon their religion. The persecution was part of his program of Hellenization, the purpose of which was to unify his sprawling empire. Many Jews gave in; others became martyrs; still others, the Maccabees, took to military resistance.

Just as modern readers of a historical novel know better than to think the fictional fill-ins are history, the ancient Jews also knew well how to interpret the genres of their culture. They knew they must discount the extremely colorful imagery to get the sober content. Even today, any attentive reader should be able to see that there is no spaceship in the Book of Daniel. Reread the quotation, and ask whether, if taken to the letter, it really describes a spaceship. The "chariots of the gods" people focus on one point and overlook the others.

Go back and read the earlier part of chapter 7 of Daniel, which tells of four great beasts that came out of the sea. One was like a lion with eagle's wings. Daniel saw its wings torn off: "it was lifted up from the ground and made to stand upon two feet like a man; and the mind of a man was given to it." Clearly we are not dealing with a spaceship here!

"And behold, another beast, a second one, like a bear," says Daniel 7:5. "It was raised up on one side; it had three ribs in its mouth between its teeth. . . . I looked and lo, another, like a leopard, with four wings of a bird on its back; and the beast had four heads." Then he saw a fourth beast with great iron teeth, and it had ten horns. Daniel saw "among them another horn, a little one, before which three of the first horns were plucked up by the roots; and behold, in this horn were eyes like the eyes of a man, and a mouth speaking great things."

Right after this comes the throne scene, after which Daniel is given the interpretation of the strange beasts. They are four kings. The ten horns are kings of the Seleucid dynasty. Antiochus gets power by getting rid of several claimants, other horns. He is the horn that speaks boastfully.

All of these images are miles away from being a spaceship! Chapter 8 of Daniel also presents visions of strange beasts, and an explanation. Still more bizarre images and visions come in chapters 9-12. Notes in the Jerusalem Bible and the American Bible explain many of the symbols. In chapter 12, we seem to have a case of multiple fulfillment (see our chapter 5).

In chapter 5 we also mentioned briefly some scriptural passages earlier than Daniel in which there is extreme imagery. Let us look at them more fully now to see how vivid were the imaginations of some of these Jewish writers.

In chapter 1 of Ezekiel the prophet, probably written in Babylonia during the exile, not long after 597 B.C., we get a very bizarre description of the throne of God. Ezekiel saw four animals of human form, and "each had four faces, and each of them had four wings. Their legs were straight and the soles of their feet were like the soles of a calf's foot; and they sparkled like burnished bronze. Under their wings on their four sides they had human hands." Here Ezekiel probably borrowed some of the strange imagery from Assyrian cherubs he had seen in Babylon.

Ezekiel adds, beginning with 1:15, "Now as I looked at the living creatures, I saw a wheel upon the earth beside the living creatures, one for each of the four of them. . . . When they went, they went in any of their four directions without turning as they went. The four wheels had rims . . . and their rims were full of eyes round about. . . . Over the head of the living creatures there was the likeness of a firmament. . . . And under the firmament their wings were stretched out straight, one toward another; and each creature had two wings covering its body. . . . And above the firmament . . . there was the likeness of a throne, in appearance like sapphire; and seated above the likeness of a throne was a likeness as it were of a human form. And upwards from what had the appearance of his loins I saw as it were gleaming bronze . . . and downward from what had the appearance of his loins I saw as it were the appearance of fire, and there was a brightness round about him, like the appearance of a bow that is in the cloud on the day of rain. . . ." This was the throne of God.

Now let anyone who wishes try to take all this at face value as a description of a spaceship. It simply does not work. It is a forerunner of Daniel's imagery.

Still other extremely colorful imagery is found in Ezekiel 32:7-8, telling of the coming divine judgment against Pharaoh: "When I blot you out, I will cover the heavens, and make their stars dark; I will cover the sun with a cloud, and the moon shall not give its light. All the bright lights of heaven will I make dark over you, and put darkness in your land." (Compare Matthew 24:29-31.)

Still earlier imagery of the same kind occurs in Isaiah 13:10, foretelling the destruction of Babylon: "For the stars of the heavens and their constellations will not give their light; the sun will be dark at its rising and the moon will not shed its light." More of the same appears in God's judgment on Edom, in Isaiah 34:4: "All the host of heaven shall rot away, and the skies roll up like a scroll."

Still earlier roots of such highly imaginative word paintings appear in Psalm 18:6-15, which seems to picture David giving thanks for his rescue from Saul, in very much overdone language: "In my distress I called upon the Lord. . . . From his temple he heard my voice. . . . Then the earth reeled and rocked; the foundations also of the mountains trembled. . . . He bowed the heavens, and came down; thick darkness was under his feet. He rode on a cherub, and flew. . . . The Lord also thundered in the heavens. . . . He made darkness his covering around him, his canopy thick clouds dark with water. . . . The Lord also thundered in the heavens. . . . And he sent out his arrows, and scattered them; he flashed forth lightnings, and routed them. Then the channels of the sea were seen, and the foundations of the world were laid bare, at thy rebuke, O Lord."

The more sober picture can be seen in 1 and 2 Samuel, telling of David's dangers and rescue. In 2 Samuel 22, David sings almost the identical thanksgiving. (God riding on the cherubim is pictured also in Psalm 80:1 and 99:1. Ezekiel 10:20 explicitly identifies the animals of chapter 1 as cherubs.)

By now one can see most clearly what folly it is to take these descriptions as spaceships. Those who think that way should look at *all* the images involved. And, of course, we have absolute evidence, independent of the Old Testament, for our God, which was summarized in chapter 2 of this book.

The last book of the New Testament is called, in Greek *Apocalypsis*, which means "Revelation." There is no doubt that it is a strong example of the apocalyptic genre. Modern commentators, however, show two quite different tendencies in treating it. Some so stress the apocalyptic genre, insisting that it is a book of consolation for all times, as to almost, if not entirely, ignore the prophetic character of some parts, that is, it contains predictions of the future. Others strongly stress the predictive aspect, some in a fundamentalistic way. The Church has said very little on the content of this book. However, there are two points on which we do have some guidance.

First, there was a millenarian or chiliastic theory, in the first centuries, which was held even by some of the Fathers of the Church, but not by enough of them to give us a proof that the theory was divinely revealed.

More precisely, there were three chief forms of this chiliasm. All started from a misunderstanding of chapter 20 of Revelation, which speaks of two resurrections; first of the just; then, of the wicked. The just were to reign with Christ on earth for a thousand years before the second resurrection.

The gross, or extreme, theory held that the just would enjoy immoderate sensory pleasures in this interval. Eusebius, in *Church History* 3:28, tells us the heretic Cerinthus, late first century, held this.

The moderate form of the theory held that the just would have sensory pleasure, but in a moderate form. Eusebius 3:39 tells us an example of this theory was found in Papias, who influenced later writers.

The mild form of the theory held that the just would enjoy spiritual pleasures. St. Justin the Martyr, in *Dialogue with Trypho*, 80, seems to hold this view; so does St. Irenaeus, in *Against Heresies*, 5.32.1. St. Augustine, in *City of God*, 20:7, says that he once held this (see his Sermon 259).

St. Augustine himself, *City of God*, 20:7-9, gives an interpretation of this part of Revelation that is widely accepted by scholars today. He says the thousand years stand for all the time from the departure of Christ at His Ascension to His return at the end, except for the brief period of the Antichrist just before the end. The just will reign during this period in that they have mastery over their own sensory desires. Otherwise, instead of reigning, they would be slaves.

In modern times a mitigated form of millenarianism was rejected by the Holy Office in a decision of July 21, 1944: "What is to be thought of the system of mitigated millenarianism which holds that Christ the Lord would come to reign visibly on this earth with or without a previous resurrection of many just persons? Reply: The system of mitigated millenarianism cannot be safely taught."

The Church has had somewhat more to say about the marvelous vision at the start of Revelation 12: "And a great portent appeared in heaven, a woman clothed with the sun, with the moon under her feet, and on her head a crown of twelve stars; she was with child and she cried out in her pangs of birth, in anguish for delivery."

A huge red dragon then appears with seven heads and ten horns. Its tail drags a third of the stars out of the sky, then it stands before the woman ready to devour her child when it would be born. Revelation continues: "she brought forth a male child, one who is to rule all nations with a rod of iron, but her child was caught up to God and to his throne, and the woman fled into the wilderness, where she has a place prepared by God, in which to be nourished for one thousand, two hundred and sixty days."

Some features fit the Virgin Mary, Mother of God. The male child who rules with the iron scepter refers to Psalm 2:9, which speaks of Christ. The child is taken up to the throne of God. Other features fit the Church, and not Mary; the pain in childbirth. St. Pius X (*Ad diem illum*, February 2, 1904: *Acta Sanctae Sedis* 36:458-459) wrote: "No one is ignorant of the fact that that woman signified the Virgin Mary, who, remaining a virgin, brought forth our Head. . . . So John saw the most Holy Mother of God already enjoying eternal happiness, and yet laboring from some hidden birth. With what birth? Surely ours, we who, being yet detained in exile, are still to be brought forth to the perfect love of God and eternal happiness."

Paul VI, in *Signum Magnum* (May 13, 1967), wrote: "The great sign that the Apostle John saw in heaven, 'a woman clothed with the sun,' is interpreted by the sacred liturgy, not without foundation, as referring to the most Blessed Mary, the mother of all men by the grace of Christ, the Redeemer."

Bernard J. Le Frois, S.V.D., in a remarkable study, *The Woman Clothed with the Sun* (Orbis Catholicus, Roma, 1954), suggests that we really have an established Semitic pattern in this passage, in which an individual stands for, and even embodies, a collectivity. Thus the woman would be Mary individually. She would stand for the Church. Le Frois further suggests that this could be a prophecy, that near the end the Church would take on a specially Marian character, resulting in a sort of age of Mary.

Chapter 14

Wisdom Literature

A powerful form of snob appeal was tempting many Christians, by the late second century, to join a bizarre group called the Gnostics. Some today are representing the Gnostics as just one of several ways of understanding Christianity, a way that happened to lose out because of superior political ability on the part of the bishops. There is almost a parallel to the Gnostic situation to be seen in some of these modern defenders of Gnosticism. One has only to look into the actual tenets of the Gnostics to see how vain is the claim that, but for politics, we might all be Gnostics today.

There were many varieties of Gnosticism. All had some things in common however. First, they had a most exalted idea of God—something missing today in many Catholics. But, sadly and secondly, they thought that matter is evil, not made by God. From God there "emanate"—they do not make clear what they mean by that word—pairs of aeons, male and female. The first pair produces the second, the second a third, and so on. As the chain stretches out, the aeons become less and less perfect. It is easy to see that sooner or later a pair would be evil. The evil ones were cast out of "the pleroma" (the full assembly of aeons). An evil aeon, the Demiurge, created man and the material world. This evil creator is the God of the Old Testament. High-sounding names abound as the Gnostics describe things: a pair is a "syzigie." For example, the syzigie Proarche and Ennoea produced Nous, who is Monogenes, and Aletheia. Then Logos and Zoe, etc., etc.

We can read the details of Gnostic thought today in works,

found in 1946-1947 at Nag Ha'amadi (Chenoboskion), in Egypt. We also have the descriptions by St. Irenaeus, in his great work *Against Heresies*, which was entirely aimed at Gnosticism.

Clement of Alexandria, head of the catechetical school at Alexandria in the late second century, decided to set up a counterattraction. He would offer courses giving a deeper understanding of Christian doctrine.

Unfortunately, in his scriptural work, Clement relied heavily on allegorical interpretation instead of trying to find out the literal sense (what the inspired writer really meant to convey—considering the genre chosen, the peculiarities of his language, culture, and so on). Allegory had deep roots at Alexandria. Jews, such as Aristobulus and Philo, had used allegory to defend the dietary laws of the Old Testament. Christian thinkers in some cases thought the literal sense unworthy of God, and so they turned to allegory. Later, St. Ambrose's use of allegory solved St. Augustine's worries about incidents in the Old Testament.

In books II and III of his *Paidagogos*, Clement tried especially to get a deeper knowledge of the rules of morality. He gave highly specific rules for how a Christian should do everything: eat, drink, sleep, dress, use sex, and so forth. He supports his injunctions with quotations from Scripture. In *Paidagogos* 2.7.58, Clement says: "I believe that one should limit his speech [at a banquet]. The limit should be just to reply to questions, even when we can speak. In a woman, silence is a virtue, and adornment free of danger in the young. Only for honored old age is speech good: 'Speak, old man, at a banquet for it is proper for you. . . . Speak, [young man], if there is need of you, scarcely, when asked twice.'"

Clement is quoting Ecclesiasticus/Sirach 32:3 and 7. Clearly he does not understand the matter of genre in Scripture. Clement seems to think the words of Ecclesiasticus are divinely revealed commands or advice on what one should do at a banquet. But Ecclesiasticus did not mean his words to be taken that way. He was writing in a genre we call wisdom literature, which aims most basically at giving worldly-wise maxims on how to get ahead in the world. He was not giving a religious injunction at all, at that point, though there are connections to religion at certain points in Israelite wisdom literature. So we need to distinguish religious injunctions from mere worldly advice in the wisdom books of Scripture. Clement failed to do that. We can see this more clearly with a bit of history of the development of wisdom literature.

Many nations wrote that kind of literature. The Egyptians were specially famed for it, as we can gather from I Kings 4:30: "Solomon's wisdom surpassed the wisdom of all the people of the east, and all the wisdom of Egypt."

The starting point of Egyptian wisdom was worldly-wise advice given by a father to a son, especially, though not exclusively, to train a successful courtier. However, there was also a connection to the religious concept of *ma'at* in Egypt. No one English word carries the full meaning of *ma'at*. John A. Wilson, in *The Culture of Ancient Egypt* (University of Chicago, 1956), writes that the word is "variously translated as 'truth,' 'justice,' 'righteousness,' 'order,' and so on. . . . *Ma'at* then, was a created and inherited rightness, which tradition built up into a concept of orderly stability . . ." (p. 48). The concept seems to be that what furthers good order and good morals is also beneficial to humanity.

St. Augustine has a similar thought in *Confessions* 1:12 when, speaking to God, he says, "For you have ordered it, and it is so, that every disordered soul is its own punishment." Similarly, St. Paul answered the licentious in Corinth who abused his teaching that they were free from the law: "'All things are lawful for me,' but not all things are helpful" (1 Corinthians 6:12).

As a result of this type of thinking, later wisdom works in the Old Testament identified wisdom and the law. So in Ecclesiasticus/Sirach 24:22-25, we read: "Whoever obeys me [wisdom] will not be put to shame, and those who work with my help will not sin. All this is the book of the covenant of the Most High God, the law which Moses commanded us as an inheritance for the congregations of Jacob. It fills men with wisdom, like the Pishon, and like the Tigris at the time of the first fruits." Similarly, Proverbs 1:7 says that "the fear of the Lord is the beginning of knowledge; fools despise wisdom and instruction."

We could add a psychological reflection. The sane man is he who sees reality as it is, and reacts appropriately. The insane man is he who sees reality as it is not. He thinks himself Napoleon, or imagines everyone is after him, and then, of course, reacts inappropriately. He who understands the advantage of serving God and acts accordingly is the most fully sane man, the wise man.

Yet as we saw, not every bit of advice in the wisdom books is a matter of divine law. Worldly wisdom suggests additional things, including some that Clement did not understand well.

There are many striking parallels between Old Testament wisdom literature and the Egyptian wisdom of Amenemopet. For example, Proverbs 15:16-17 reads: "Better is a little with fear of the Lord than great treasure and trouble with it. Better is a dinner of herbs where love is than a fatted ox and hatred with it." Amenemopet says: "Better is poverty in the hand of the god than riches within a storehouse. Better is bread, when the heart is happy, than riches with sorrow." Proverbs 22:17 to 24:22 is especially close to Amenemopet. For example, Proverbs 22:17-18 says, "Incline your ear, and hear the words of the wise, and apply your mind to my knowledge; for it will be pleasant if you keep them within you, if all of them are ready on your lips." Amenemopet says: "Give thy ears. Hear what is said, give thy heart to understand them. To put them in thy heart is worth while, but it is damaging to him who neglects them."[1]

The Book of Proverbs consists mostly of short, pithy sayings and has little continuity. The sayings represent much of the worldly-wise wisdom aspect of wisdom literature, though 1:7 makes the tie to religion: "The fear of the Lord is the beginning of knowledge." The book opens by claiming to be "the proverbs of Solomon, son of David, king of Israel." This does not mean that the whole book must be attributed to Solomon. The Israelites, as was said before, often used pen names, frequently preferring the name of a famous man. Solomon's renown for wisdom led to such attributions. It is quite possible that parts of this book may really stem from Solomon. Chapters 10-29 are probably from before the great Exile. On the other hand, the long prologue is apt to come from the fifth century B.C.

Israel made use of wisdom found in other nations. Thus chapter 30 of Proverbs is entitled "The words of Agur son of Jakeh of Massa." Massa is the name of an Ishmaelite tribe in north Arabia that was thought to have the wisdom of the East. Chapter 31 opens: "The words of Lemuel, king of Massa, which his mother taught him." (It is not certain that *Massa* was meant as a proper name. The word might mean an oracle or prophecy.)

Proverbs ends with a beautiful alphabetic poem on the ideal wife. We do not know when or by whom it was composed. Recall that in the ancient Near East, rights of authorship were not insisted on; later hands might make additions. Thus several inspired authors may have contributed to this work. When they use wisdom from outside Israel, they do so because they judge it good, either in the worldly-wise sense, or in the religious sense.

Ecclesiasticus/Sirach is in many ways similar to Proverbs in that it includes many pithy sayings. Yet there is in Sirach some grouping by ideas, even though one could hardly make a logical outline of the book as a whole. Yet the book was probably written centuries later than Proverbs. Probably composed in the second century B.C., it, too, includes a strong religious aspect.

There are some lines in the Book of Proverbs that raise questions about the afterlife (see our discussion in chapter 7). Clearly, though the writer did not know the answers we know, he nonetheless did not teach any error. Those answers finally appear in the Book of Wisdom. For example in 3:1-3 we read: "But the souls of the righteous are in the hand of God, and no torment will ever touch them. In the eyes of the foolish they seemed to have died, and their departure was thought to be an affliction, and their going from us to be their destruction; but they are at peace."

The Book of Job earlier had wrestled mightily with the problem of the just man meeting great affliction. It seems in a way to have given the answer in the last lines (42:10-17). Job was rewarded richly before his death. Yet the more substantial answer of the book seems to be to bow down trustingly before the inscrutable majesty of God. The author of the Book of Ecclesiasticus, Qoheleth, too, had struggled mightily. Seeing the emptiness of all earthly things, he added not a few lines that seem to point ahead, though not clearly, to future retribution.

But by the time the Book of Wisdom was written, probably in the first century B.C., Israel's thought had been divinely guided into an agonizing reappraisal. The Israelites knew that God acted justly, but their eyes told them that not always do things work out rightly in this life. Yet their realization of future retribution was dim at best. So, they without being able to see, were called on to hold to God in heroic faith. The agonizing reappraisal was probably sparked by the dreadful deaths of the martyrs under Antiochus Epiphanes. One could not say that they were repaid before their deaths! The reappraisal of their thinking was aided, perhaps, by contact with Greek thought, in which the twofold nature of man, body and soul, showed better how to find room for future retribution.

We saw above that wisdom came to be equated with the law. In a further stage, wisdom is personified. Wisdom 9:9-18 says: "With thee is wisdom, who knows thy works and was present when thou didst make the world, and who understands what is pleasing in thy sight. . . . Send her forth from the holy heavens, and from the throne of thy glory send her, that she may be with me and toil, and that I may learn what is pleasing to thee. For she knows and understands all things. . . . For the reasoning of mortals is worthless . . . for a perishable body weighs down the soul, and this earthly tent burdens the thoughtful mind. We can hardly guess at what is on earth . . . but who has traced out what is in the heavens? Who has learned thy counsel, unless thou has given wisdom and sent thy Holy Spirit from on high? And thus the paths of those on earth were set right, and men were taught what pleases thee, and were saved by wisdom." (In the Old Testament, "Holy Spirit" means a power that comes forth from God, not the Third Divine Person, for the Holy Trinity had not yet been revealed.)

Chapter 15

Variant Traditions

How did David come to meet King Saul? There is a fascinating problem in the First Book of Samuel, in chapters 16 and 17.

In 16:14 and following, we find Saul tormented by an evil spirit. Much distressed, Saul asks his servants to find a man skilled at playing the harp to soothe him. They find David (16:18), "a son of Jesse the Bethlehemite, who is skillful in playing, a man of valor, a man of war, prudent in speech. . . ." So David enters his service. "And Saul loved him greatly, and he became his armor-bearer. And Saul sent to Jesse saying, 'Let David remain in my service.'"

But in chapter 17 of First Samuel, David seems not to be in the service of Saul; he is feeding his father's sheep. One day when his father sends him to bring food to his brothers who are in the army, David hears of Goliath the giant and of the great reward the king offers to the one who will conquer Goliath. So David goes to Saul and, boasting of having killed lions and bears, offers to fight Goliath. Saul gives David armor, but David is not used to wearing it and discards it. He goes instead against Goliath with a sling and some stones from the brook. Yet in 16:18, quoted above, David was a mighty fighter, a *gibbor*. Also in 17:55, one may read: "When Saul saw David go forth against the Philistine, he said to Abner, the commander of the army, 'Abner, whose son is this youth?' And Abner said, 'As your soul lives, O king, I cannot tell.'" But chapter 16 has just said that David had been in Saul's service as his armor-bearer.

It is difficult, perhaps impossible, to reconcile the two accounts. The oldest Greek translation of the Book of Samuel simply omitted the second account.

How can we defend the correctness of Scripture at a point like this? We already know the answer. The key to the problem is to ask, *What did the inspired writer mean to assert?* Yes, the Books of Samuel are basically in the genre of history, it seems. Yet let us try to visualize the situation. The inspired writer is sitting down at his desk and working on the First Book of Samuel. He has before him several sources. We saw already, in our chapter 3, that there are likely to be such sources in the Pentateuch.

But the inspired writer runs into a problem. He has two sources on hand for this incident that do not fit together. He undoubtedly tries to find out which is correct, but he can't. What would he be likely to do in this situation? He might well decide to give us both versions. This solution fits with his purpose of showing how God favors the Israelites when they are faithful, punishes them when they are unfaithful.

If the inspired writer does give us both versions—as he has—what does he *assert*? Clearly both versions cannot be correct. In giving the two versions, the inspired writer is, in effect, telling us: "I found these two versions. I do not know which is correct. But here they are." So there is no error at all.

Another example of the same sort of thing is found in the accounts of the crossing of the Red Sea in the Book of Exodus. Most of us have seen the dramatic movie *The Ten Commandments* in which can be seen a high wall of water on both sides of the Israelites as they cross on the dry sea bottom. At the appropriate moment, the waters return to drown the Egyptian army.

Chapter 14 of Exodus seems to be a weaving together of two different versions. Exodus 14:21-25 says: "Then Moses stretched out his hand over the sea; and the Lord drove the sea back by a strong wind all night, and made the sea dry land, and the waters were divided. And the people of Israel went into the midst of the sea on dry ground, the waters being a wall to them on their right and on their left." A wind drying up the sea at night would not yield a wall of water on both right and left, the scene in the well-known movie.

The passage continues: "The Egyptians pursued, and went in after them into the midst of the sea. . . . And in the morning watch the Lord in the pillar of fire and of cloud looked down upon the host of the

Egyptians, and discomfited the host of the Egyptians, clogging their chariot wheels so that they drove heavily; and the Egyptians said 'Let us flee from before Israel; for the Lord fights for them against the Egyptians.'"

Here the description seems to hark back to the idea of a dried up sea bottom that could clog the chariot wheels. But, then, Exodus 14:26-29 says: "The Lord said to Moses, 'Stretch out your hand over the sea, that the water may come back upon the Egyptians'. . . . The waters returned and covered the chariots and the horsemen and all the host of Pharaoh that had followed them into the sea; not so much as one of them remained."

The answer, of course, is the same as in the case of David's meeting Saul. The inspired writer had on hand two versions, did not know which was the correct one, and gave us both.

This time the inspired writer not only gave both but intertwined them closely together. One reason he may have decided to do this was the genre of the Book of Exodus. It is quite probable that the genre was intended to be at least something like epic.

Epic genre was well known in the ancient Near East and among many other peoples too. In it there is an account in which the historically accurate core is embellished with poetic exaggerations. Pius XII, in *Divino Afflante Spiritu* (1943), spoke of this fact: "No one who has the right idea of biblical inspiration will be surprised that in Sacred Scripture, just as in other ancient works, there are found certain ways of expression and narration, certain definite idiomatic things, proper especially to the Semitic languages: so-called approximations, and certain hyperbolic ways of speaking, at times even paradoxes, by which the matter is more firmly imprinted in the mind."

The Pope adds a further explanation: "For just as the substantial Word of God became like to men in all things 'without sin' [Hebrews 4:15], so also the words of God expressed in human tongues, are made like human speech in all things except error. St. John Chrysostom highly praised this *synkatabasis*, that is, condescension [adaptation to human ways] and over and over again said it was found in Sacred Books."

It is quite probable that the Book of Joshua is also in something like epic genre. We can see this particularly when we compare the general picture of Joshua with that given in Judges.

In the Book of Joshua we have a brilliant picture: all of Israel is united under one leader, Joshua. There are many miracles. Their armies go from one victory to another, until practically all of the land has been subdued: the people of Canaan have been virtually eliminated, their cities burned. And the land has been divided among the tribes and the covenant renewed. After all of this Joshua dies at a ripe old age.

Incidentally, God willed the wipe-out of the Canaanites for two reasons: (1) to guard against the danger that the Israelites might fall into idolatry under their influence—a thing that really happened, for the victory was not nearly so complete; (2) to punish the Canaanites for their sins. Recall to mind Genesis 15:16, in which God promised to give the whole land to Abraham and his descendants but said that it would not happen at once: "And they shall come back here in the fourth generations; for the iniquity of the Amorites [west Semites] is not yet complete."

God of course is the master of all land and of all lives. He did not need to wait for their sins to reach the maximum before taking away their land. Yet His Holiness willed to do it that way, so that they might most fully deserve their fate. Some today are shocked at God's reported orders of extermination. They forget that He is the giver of life and has no obligation to continue to give it beyond any point He fixes. And when immense sins intervene, He has an added reason for terminating lives.

But to return to the Book of Joshua, the picture is epic idealization. Contrast this with the picture in the Book of Judges, which is not idealized. We soon see in it that the conquest had been far from complete. Yet there is no error. Again our study of the differences in genres makes clear what the inspired writers meant to assert.

There are other examples of variant traditions in the Old Testament that can be explained in the same way. A probable example is the narrative of Saul's rejection by God as king of the Hebrews so that his dynasty would go no further. One of these examples, in 1 Samuel 13:1-14, tells how Saul did not wait for Samuel but offered sacrifice himself before battle. The other, in 15:1-31, tells how Saul in fighting against Agag, king of Amalek, doomed only the worthless. Samuel told him, "Behold, to obey is better than sacrifice, and to hearken than the fat of rams" (15:22). It is just possible that the events in these two passages could both have happened.

Incidentally, someone may wonder why God refused to forgive Saul when, in 15:24, he begged for forgiveness, whereas God did forgive King David later when he asked forgiveness for murder and adultery (2 Samuel 11:1-12:15). The answer is found in a distinction between two orders, the internal order of eternal salvation and the external order, which deals with the position a man may have. God always forgives the repentant sinner in the external order.

We have now seen, in several chapters, many applications of the approach through literary genres. We have seen that it enables us to reject claims of error or contradiction in Scripture, many of which problems would otherwise be unsolvable.

The fact raises an interesting problem: it is only in our century that this approach in terms of literary genres became known. It was only in 1943 that Pope Pius XII, in *Divino Afflante Spiritu*, positively encouraged the Church to use it. We saw, in chapter 9, there was a very qualified acceptance of the genre approach by the Biblical Commission in 1905. But the Church had been interpreting Scripture for many centuries without knowing about literary genres the way we do. So we must ask: Did not the Church make many mistakes in her teaching through lack of this knowledge of genres?

No, the Church made no mistake in her teaching for lack of this knowledge; but yes, this approach has given us further light, especially since it enables us to answer many objections against Scripture, charges of error or contradiction, which could not be answered before. But there has been no mistake in teaching.

How can this inerrancy be explained? There are two answers. First, the Church enjoys the promised protection of the Holy Spirit. Even if the Church did not know many things, the Spirit always does, and He guides the Church.

The second answer is that the Church has something even more basic than Scripture. What that is and how it works, we will begin to explore in chapter 20.

Chapter 16

Demise of Historical-Critical Method?

Strange indeed is the view that meets our eyes today as we survey the landscape of Scripture studies. The historical-critical method, which for centuries has reigned as queen, is now being cast out bodily—not by all, but by many of the most prominent scholars. These scholars are turning instead to structuralism, psychoanalytic readings of the Gospels, sociological interpretation, and other things. More on these points later. For now, let us look at the historical-critical method itself.

As its name indicates, the historical-critical method is an approach to Scripture within the framework of history. It is demanding, takes nothing for granted, and seemingly requires solid proof for its findings. The use of literary genres is a major part of the historical-critical method. Its other chief components are: textual criticism, source criticism, form and redaction criticism. A brief survey of the early stages of the historical-critical method will be useful at this point.

Although the method in general belongs to recent centuries, there were some forerunners. St. Augustine, for instance, knew that we must not suppose God made an actual image of clay for the first man, since God does not have bodily hands (*De Genesi ad litteram* 6.12.20). St. John Chrysostom, in *On Genesis*, warned against taking the rib-to-Eve episode crudely. Theodore of Mopsuestia was considered rationalistic because he understood that the Canticle of Canticles is romance lyric. Hugh of St. Victor denied that Solomon wrote the Book of Wisdom.

93

Rabbi Ibn Ezra of Toledo, in the twelfth century, raised historical problems in Genesis.

Turning to the Old Testament specifically, we find that a priest, Richard Simon (1638-1712), thought that a group of "public secretaries" gradually added to the first five books of the Bible up to the time of Ezra (fifth century B.C.). A Protestant, H. B. Witter, in 1711, was the first to suggest that different names for God (Elohim/Yahweh Elohim) could point to different documents. A Catholic, J. Astruc, in 1753, was the first to divide Genesis into various documents, partly on the basis of the difference in divine names. Karl Ilgen, in 1798, asserted that the Elohist source was really two sources: E^1 and E^2. Today these are usually called E and P (for Priestly Code).

Others, such as Alexander Geddes (1792), Johann Vater (1771-1826), and William de Wette (1780-1849), were unconvinced of the documentary theory. Instead they proposed that many fragments had been put together by an editor in the time of Solomon, or even Hezekiah. H. Ewald (1805-1875) said there was one basic document—he called it *Grundschrift* ("basic writing")—which was E, and that gaps were filled in from a J (source using Yahweh) in the times of Saul, Solomon, and Ezekiel. Still later, Ewald redivided E (Elohist document). When E. Riehm, in 1854, solidly established D (Deuteronomist) as a separate document, there was a rebirth of the documentary theory in its basically modern form, which supposes four documents: J, E, P, and D.

Julius Wellhausen (1844-1918), working especially in the study of law, refined these theories. He thought the Pentateuch (first five books) and Joshua reached their present form after the Exile, at the time of Ezra, around 450 B.C.

But we need to notice especially two currents that had been present for some time in Old Testament studies: a tendency to deny the supernatural, and a tendency to fit everything into a mold suggested by the German philosopher Hegel. Let us look at each of these.

H. Reimaurus (1694-1768) asserted that the Old Testament is myth and that the New Testament contains deliberate falsification by disciples of Jesus. J. G. Eichhorn (1752-1827) disagreed but nonetheless held that there was nothing supernatural in the Old Testament. Primitive peoples, unable to recognize secondary causes, he reasoned, attributed everything to God directly.

G. W. F. Hegel (1770-1831) held that man progresses through recurring cycles of conflict and resolution: someone takes a position; a counterposition arises; out of their interaction comes a third position (thesis, antithesis, synthesis). In line with this tendency. W. Vatke (1806-1881) thought that religion became revealed slowly through stages of simile, allegory, myth, Christianity. The Bible, he held, is more a history of man's consciousness than a record of past events. A fully objective biblical theology, he said, can never exist. This position led, of course, to a devaluation of the Old Testament, which tendency was furthered by F. Schleiermacher (1768-1834), who made religion a matter of sentiment rather than knowledge. Julius Wellhausen, mentioned above, was successful not so much for radically new views as for a logical and cogent presentation of the ideas of his predecessors. He, too, followed Hegel, through the influence of Vatke, and rejected all supernatural elements in the religion of Israel.

Even this sketchy survey of some of the principal writers about the Old Testament easily shows us the immense amount of prejudice (rejection of all supernatural things without proof), the subjectivism, the insufficiently proved theories that run so strongly in the works on the Pentateuch. Studies of other parts of the Old Testament, especially the prophets, are also characterized by these kinds of defects.

New Testament criticism in some ways is even more dismal. Here, too, we see early the baneful influence of what people in their conceit called "the Enlightenment" in the eighteenth century. These "enlightened" thinkers denied the supernatural, denied anything beyond human reason, said that mysteries of faith could be explained away by reason. Then, of course, divine revelation would neither be needed nor given. God was adequately manifested in nature. Miracles are impossible, since physical laws are the expression of the unchangeable will of God.

The same H. S. Reimaurus, in *The Aims of Jesus and His Disciples* (1778), distinguished the historical Jesus from the Christ of the Gospels—what He really was, from what His disciples told about Him. The real Jesus was a revolutionary who tried to start an earthly messianic kingdom but failed. The disciples stole the body, invented the Resurrection and the expectation of His return (the parousia). Then they changed the idea of messiahship to a spiritual one.

Johann Michaelis (1717-1791), not knowing how to solve the problem of which books are inspired, said that only those inspired by the Apostles were inspired. Mark and Luke, thus, are not inspired, but the fanciful apocryphal Gospels (under the names of James, Philip, Thomas, etc.) are inspired.

H. E. G. Paulus (1761-1851) reacted against the claims of gross fraud. He said the disciples were not dishonest, just too simple. Miracles could all be explained in terms of natural causes. People mistook natural events for miracles.

David F. Strauss (1808-1874) really shook the world with his two-volume *Life of Jesus Critically Examined* (1835-1836). He said the Gospels were written in the middle of the second century, to give time for myth to develop. He said that the records were based on Old Testament episodes, later applied to the Messiah (compare R. E. Brown's *The Birth of the Messiah*).

F. C. Baur (1792-1860) exerted great influence. Using Hegel again, Baur supposed a confrontation between a Petrine Jewish faction and a Pauline faction. The outcome was "Early Catholicism." We could date New Testament writings, Baur thought, by noticing which tendency—the Pauline or the Petrine—is represented in a given book.

The real founder of liberal Protestantism was A. Ritschl (1822-1889), who held that religious judgments are value judgments based only on feelings of approval or disapproval. Whether or not they have any objective reality is not important, nor can we know. Here, again, we have a distinction between the Jesus of history and the Christ of faith.

W. Wrede, whose work is still very influential, in *The Messianic Secret* (1901), said that Jesus never claimed to be the Messiah; later the Church was embarrassed by His silence and so covered by faking scenes in the Gospels in which He would tell people to keep quiet about the fact that He was the Messiah.

Most of these unfortunate interpretations of Scripture came out of Germany. England produced "the Cambridge Three," who countered the "liberal" views. J. B. Lightfoot (1828-1889), studied early writings, especially the Epistle of Pope Clement I and the letters of St. Ignatuis of Antioch. Lightfoot showed that they were, respectively, works of the late first and early second centuries. This pushed back Gospel dating from the middle of the second century, since these writings do quote the Gospels. And they showed there was no drawn out conflict of Petrine and Pauline factions as Baur had supposed. The other two of the Cambridge Three, Westcott and Hort, also wrote commentaries, but their great production was a critical text of the Greek New Testament, replacing the inadequate old *textus receptus*, which was based on poor manuscript evidence.

Reginald H. Fuller, one of the leading Protestant form critics, in his review of *The Birth of the Messiah*, by Raymond Brown, chided Brown: "It is ironic that just at the time when the limitations of the historical-critical method are being discovered in Protestantism, Roman Catholic scholars should be bent on pursuing that method so relentlessly" (*Catholic Biblical Quarterly* 40, 1978, p. 120). That was written in 1978.

By 1980, the same R. H. Fuller had said that the method was bankrupt (*St. Luke's Journal of Theology* 23, 1980, p. 96), and that the bankruptcy should be overcome by feedback from the believing community. Walter Wink had said much the same in *The Bible in Human Transformation* (Philadelphia: Fortress, 1973, p. 1).

The historical-critical method is by nature limited, since the kind of evidence it can work with is almost always internal, not external. A scholar tries, for example, to find indications *within* the text telling where the Gospel of Matthew was written. Meier argues that it was written at Antioch (*Antioch and Rome*, Raymond E. Brown and John P. Meier, Paulist, 1983, pp. 12-72). He thinks that the confrontation between Peter and Paul (Galatians 2:11-14) was so heated that, as a result, Paul seldom went back to Antioch thereafter. Martin Hengel (*Acts and the History of Earliest Christianity*, tr. John Bowden, Philadelphia: Fortress, 1979, p. 122) seems to think the same, for he speaks of a "momentous clash between Paul and the advocates of the 'synthesis' (Gal. 2.11ff.)." But there is no proof that Peter held to an unwillingness to follow the doctrinal decision of the Council of Jerusalem (Acts 15:7ff.), in which Peter himself had taken the lead in agreeing with Paul that gentile converts need not observe the Mosaic law.

As to Barnabas, Acts 15:36-40 says that Paul did suggest to Barnabas that he come on a second missionary expedition. Though he was willing, "Barnabas wanted to take with them John called Mark. But Paul thought best not to take with them one who had withdrawn from them in Pamphylia and had not gone with them to the work" (15:37-38). Rather naturally, Paul did not favor one who had deserted, for whatever reason. Because Barnabas insisted on taking Mark, Paul and Barnabas went separately.

There is no proof at all that Peter continued in his attitude. It is much more likely that Peter had just become weak again, as he did more than once in the Gospels. Weakness would hardly make him hold on firmly to rejecting the decision of the Council of Jerusalem, in which he had taken the lead. Really, Meier seems to be resurrecting the old notion of a prolonged conflict between Peter and Paul.

So we can begin to see what R. H. Fuller meant by the "limitations" of the historical-critical method: it seldom strictly *proves* anything. But for a long time scholars did not see the limitations. Instead they would build one inconclusive thing on another and, in their cockiness, even claim for their researches the assured results of science. Now they are waking up to see what they should have seen long ago. Instead of correcting their defective judgment and using the method for what it is worth—which is considerable—they are now showing still another effect of bad judgment. At first it led them to excess confidence, now it leads to excess diffidence, to throwing out the baby with the bath water. (Examples of the method are given in chapters 17 and 18.)

Chapter 17

Vatican II on the Historical-Critical Method

St. Augustine, when he was 19, fell into the bizarre errors of Manichaeism. He soon found that Manichaean explanations of the sun and moon did not square with the astronomy of his day. So he did a prudent thing. He consulted the local Manichaean authorities. They could not solve his problems, but they said that a great bishop, Faustus, would be coming in time, and that he would explain everything.

For nine years Augustine waited. But when Faustus came, he could not answer Augustine's difficulties either. Then Augustine paid Faustus a fine compliment: "He knew that he did not know those things. . . . He was not altogether ignorant of his ignorance" (*Confessions* 5.7). If Faustus, or anyone, could always know that he did not know when he did not know, he would have an infallibility greater than that of the Pope: he would never make a false statement.

As we saw, modern practitioners of the historical-critical method have all too often not resembled Faustus. They have been too cocky, claiming scientific certitude in matters of opinion.

Vatican II, in its *Constitution on Divine Revelation*, if taken seriously, has two statements that could prevent errors of many kinds. "The task of authoritatively interpreting the word of God," it says, "whether written or handed on, has been entrusted exclusively to the living Magisterium of the Church, whose authority is exercised in the name of Jesus Christ" (n. 10).

Many scholars scream that the Church should listen to them. Otherwise, they claim, the Church is undemocratic and interferes with academic freedom. Now, of course, Church authorities should and do check to see what scholars uncover in the field of Scripture. The final judgment, however, depends, not on scholarship, but on the providentially protected magisterium. We trust the magisterium, the teaching authority of the Church, because of the promises of Christ (see chapter 2).

A specially glaring case of the opposite way of working appears in *Consensus in Theology?* (ed. Leonard Swidler, Westminster, Philadelphia, 1980). Most of the nineteen contributors to this work, many of them Catholic, are in substantial agreement with the featured writer, Hans Kueng, who says that there are two poles, or sources, of Christian theology. "The first . . . is God's revelational address on the history of Israel and the history of Jesus" (p. 5). This means, of course, the Old and New Testaments. "The second," says Kueng, "is our own human world of experience" (p. 11).

The teaching of the Church is simply omitted, not mentioned at all as a source of Christian theology. Instead, we should use the Bible, plus human experience, as the two sources. As to the Bible, Kueng says: "The criterion determining all other criteria of Christian theology can never again be some ecclesiastical or theological tradition or institution but only the Gospel, the original Christian message itself . . . analyzed by historical-critical analysis" (p. 14). Many Protestant critics today are saying that the historical-critical method is "bankrupt," as we saw in chapter 16. Since the method is bankrupt, they argue, it is to be supplemented, as R. H. Fuller puts it, by "feedback received from the believing community." That is, of course, the same as Kueng's "human world of experience."

The Vatican has quite rightly declared that Kueng is not a Catholic theologian at all. Kueng, as we just saw, rejects the idea that God's providence protects the teaching Church from error. He prefers private judgment, which is a purely Protestant approach to Scripture. Numerous Catholic scholars are also following private judgment. A sad instance of this can be seen in the symposium edited by a Catholic, Leonard Swidler, *Consensus in Theology?* mentioned above, in which Rosemary Reuther says Kueng is calling for this: "that the academy replace the hierarchy as the teaching magisterium of the Church. . . . It entails the equivalent of the French Revolution in the Church." Far more Catholic in the same volume is the paper by a Muslim, Seyyed Hossein Nasr, who asks what protection there is for the truth: "In Christianity it has always been the *magisterium..*"

Yet scholars do not merely repeat the magisterium, nor must they always wait for a statement. Vatican II said that "Catholic exegetes and others who cultivate Sacred Theology . . . should work so that, under the *vigilance* [emphasis added] of the Sacred Magisterium, they may, with apt helps, so investigate and present the divine letters that as many ministers of the divine word as possible may be able to effectively provide the nourishment of the Scriptures for the people of God" (n. 23).

An earlier version, finally rejected by the Council, had *lead* instead of *vigilance*. But the Council did not want to close off originality to scholars. Yet scholars must remember that their work is merely "preparatory" (n. 12) to the judgment of the Church, which is a final criterion.

Vatican II adds a further important provision, in *On Revelation* (n. 12): "But since Sacred Scripture is also to be read and interpreted by the same Spirit by which it was written, to rightly extract the sense of the sacred texts, we must look not less diligently at the content and unity of all Scripture, taking into account the living tradition of the whole Church and analogy of faith."

If, as we have established, the principal author of *all* parts of Scripture is the Holy Spirit, there can be no contradiction of one part by another. There can, however, be differences—short of real contradiction—between one Gospel and another, in outlook, scope, intention. In view of this statement of Vatican II, of course, we cannot approve of the notion of W. Harrington (*Consensus in Theology?*, p. 43) that Mary was outside the circle of salvation.

A novel claim of a clash in Scripture appears in R. Brown, *The Churches the Apostles Left Behind*, (p. 21). He compares three passages. He notices that Ephesians 2:11-22 speaks of Jesus as the one who "broke down the obstacle of the wall" between Jews and Gentiles, so that Jew and Gentile have been reconciled, joined in one body to God through the cross. But Acts 28:25-29 tells how Paul, after seeing that Jews in Rome would not listen, said that the words of Isaiah 6:9ff. applied to them: seeing they would not see, hearing they would not hear. Their heart was gross. They were permanently closed off from salvation, according to the objection. The third passage is in Romans 11:11-16, where Paul speaks of the original People of God, the Jews, as a tame olive tree, and the Gentiles as a wild olive tree. Branches were broken off the tame tree. Into their place, branches (Gentiles) from the wild tree were engrafted. Paul speaks of this entry of the Gentiles as a possible means of making the Jews jealous, and predicts that finally the Jews will be converted to Christ.

The alleged triple clash is really a triple lack of perception. The complete and true picture is this. In Romans 11:11-26, Paul pictures a tame olive tree (the original People of God), and a wild olive tree (the Gentiles). Many of the branches of the tame tree were broken off, that is, they rejected Christ and, thus, were unfaithful. In those places, the Gentiles were engrafted to form one People of God—the people envisioned in Ephesians 2:11-22. This people is formed of two groups: Gentiles plus a *remnant* of converted Jews who accepted Christ. But *the majority* of Jews are broken-off branches, that is, they have rejected Christ and, therefore, lost their places among the People of God. The Jews who dismayed Paul in Rome were the Jews who rejected Christ, though a few Jews in Rome accepted Him.

In brief, there are three groups: (1) unfaithful Jews who rejected Christ and are outside the People of God as a result, (2) a smaller group, a remnant of Jews who did accept Christ and form part of the one People of God, and (3) the converted Gentiles. So there is no clash at all.

In the quote above from Vatican II, we saw that in interpreting Scripture we must take into account "the living tradition of the whole Church and the analogy of faith." This means that a proposed interpretation that would clash with anything in the teachings of the Church is to be rejected, even if the Church has not yet spoken directly and explicitly on the passage under consideration. In this connection, some have misunderstood Pius XII, who said, in *Divino Afflante Spiritu*, that there are few texts "whose meaning has been declared by the authority of the Church, nor are there more on which there is a unanimous view of the Holy Fathers" of the early centuries. This is, of course, true. But even if the Church has not spoken *directly and explicitly* on many texts, and even if the Fathers have not been unanimous on many, yet *indirectly* we find much guidance by comparing proposed interpretations with all the truths taught by the Church. Hence Pius XII points out that we must check with the analogy of faith, as Leo XIII also told us in *Providentissimus Deus*. Commenting on texts not yet directly interpreted by the Church or by the Fathers in unanimity, Pope Leo said that "the analogy of faith must be followed. . . . Hence it is clear that an interpretation is to be rejected as inept and false which either makes the inspired authors, as it were, fight among themselves, or is opposed to a teaching of the Church."

By following this guide, practitioners of the historical-critical method can obtain better results and avoid countless errors. Further, when we say that we must reject any interpretation that would clash with any teaching of the Church, we must not confine ourselves to solemn definitions. For Vatican II (*Constitution on the Church*, n. 25) tells us that there are three levels of Church teaching, all of them mandatory. In addition, paragraph 12 speaks of the "passive infallibility" of the believing Church.

The first of the three levels is that of the solemn definition by the Holy Father. "His definitions of themselves, and not from consent of the Church," says Vatican II, "are rightly called unchangeable, for they are given under the assistance of the Holy Spirit promised him in blessed Peter; and so they need no approval of others, nor do they allow an appeal to any other judgment." Even with collegiality (of which the Council spoke in n. 23) the pope can act entirely alone when he so wills, even in defining.

The second level of Church teaching is this: "Even though individual bishops do not enjoy the prerogative of infallibility, they can still proclaim the doctrine of Christ infallibly, even when scattered throughout the world, if, keeping the bond of union among themselves and with the Successor of Peter, in teaching authoritatively on faith and morals they agree on one view as the one to be held definitively." This means that the *ordinary* magisterium of the Church, giving the day-to-day teaching of the Church definitively throughout the world, is infallible.

On the third level, the Council wrote, "Religious submission of will and of mind is to be shown in a special way to the authentic Magisterium of the Roman Pontiff, even when he is not defining."

The Council also said, "The entire body of the faithful, anointed as they are by the Holy One, cannot err in matters of belief" (n. 12). This means that if the whole Church, people as well as authorities, has—even for one period of history—accepted a teaching as revealed, that belief of the Church cannot be in error.

A rather obvious instance of such a universal belief would be the existence of angels. It has become fashionable today to deny them because in some Old Testament passages (for example, Judges 6) we find practically an alternation of expressions. Sometimes it is said that the

Lord spoke; other times, that the angel of the Lord spoke. Hence a question: Was the expression "angel of the Lord" just a literary devise meaning simply God? There are three answers.

First, it is a basic principle of Scripture study that we must get into the thought world of the original readers. But the original readers of the Old Testament, at least in the later period, and those of the New Testament as well, clearly did understand that there are separate beings called angels. Second, even though the Church has not defined the existence of angels, yet it has taught their existence on the second level mentioned by Vatican II. Third, the believing Church for centuries has taken it as revealed that there are angels.

So the Church gives us a rich abundance of guidance in our use of the historical-critical method. If we follow the rules of Vatican II, we can safely study Scripture by means of this method.

Chapter 18

Two Saint Pauls?

Of major importance are the claims, common today, that there are two conflicting images of St. Paul in Scripture: one in his Epistles, the other in the Acts of the Apostles. These claims lead, in turn, to proposing a late date for the Acts of the Apostles, and to saying that Luke, or the author of Acts, could not have been a follower of St. Paul. Hence, the two Pauls claim leads to a devaluation of the reliability of Luke's Gospel.

In chapter 16 we mentioned that scholars who use the historical-critical method are prone to reject external evidence. External evidence is found in such things as testimonies by other ancient writers, who tell us that Luke was a companion of St. Paul and that he wrote Acts. (It is generally agreed, even by radical critics, that the same person wrote both Luke and Acts.) For example, the Anti-Marcionite Prologues to the Gospels, which date from between 160 and 180 A.D., tell us: "Luke of Antioch in Syria, a physician, having become a disciple of the Apostles, and later followed Paul until his martyrdom . . . after the Gospels had been written—by Matthew in Judea, by Mark in Italy—moved by the Holy Spirit, wrote this Gospel in Achaia . . . with great care, for Gentile believers."

St. Irenaeus, Bishop of Lyons, who died probably as a martyr about 200 A.D. and who had heard St. Polycarp in Smyrna tell what he himself had heard from the Apostle St. John, tells us that "Luke, the follower of Paul, set down in a book the Gospel preached by him [Paul]" (*Against Heresies* 3.1.1).

But the critics brush aside these testimonies, preferring instead to rely exclusively upon evidence found within Scripture itself. Because of the special importance of the claim that there are two Pauls, it is important to consider the question of internal evidence in some detail. A. J. Mattill has provided a convenient summary of the arguments of the critics in his article "The Value of Acts as a Source for the Study of Paul." (In *Perspectives on Luke-Acts*, Charles H. Talbert, ed., Danville, Virginia, 1978, pp. 76-98, esp. 87-95.)

"The school of Creative Edification," writes Mattill, "finds anti-Pauline traditions in Acts. For example . . ., 9:20-22 is directed against Galatians ('straightway' of 9:20 is aimed at Gal. 1:16; 'destroyed' of 9:21 is influenced by Gal. 1:23)."

We read in Acts 9:20-22: "And in the synagogues immediately [or *straightway*—right after his conversion in Damascus] he proclaimed Jesus saying, 'He is the Son of God.' And all who heard him were amazed, and said, 'Is not this the man who made havoc in Jerusalem of those who called on this name? And he has come here for this purpose, to bring them bound before the chief priests.' But Saul increased all the more in strength. . . ." This is supposed to clash with Galatians 1:16, which says (we quote from 15 and 16): "But when he who set me apart before I was born . . . was pleased to reveal his Son to me, in order that I might preach him among the Gentiles, I did not confer with flesh and blood. . . ." In saying he did not "confer with flesh and blood," Paul merely means that he had no need to learn Christ from the Apostles or others. He had learned the truth directly from the vision on the road. So there is no problem.

The second item, "destroyed," in RSV reads "made havoc." It means Paul had greatly persecuted Christians in Jerusalem. That says the same as Galatians 1:23: "He who once persecuted us is now preaching the faith he once tried to destroy." Again, no clash.

Also on page 92 of *Perspectives on Luke-Acts*, we read that "Luke does not think of Paul as a witness of the resurrection but places in his mouth words which Paul himself would have repudiated (13-31)." Acts 13:31 says that "for many days he [Christ] appeared to those who came up with him from Galilee to Jerusalem, who are now his witnesses to the people." But Paul agreed in 1 Corinthians 15:5-8. Paul enumerated several appearances of the risen Jesus. They were witnesses to the Resurrection, not in seeing the tomb opened, but in seeing Jesus afterwards. Paul, according to Acts, had also seen Jesus afterwards, in the Damascus road vision, of which Paul also speaks in 1 Corinthians 15:8.

Again on page 92, Mattill says that "Acts 15:1-35 represents an understanding of Paul's relationship to the Jerusalem apostolate which Paul himself corrects in Gal. 2:1-10." Acts 15 tells of the Council of Jerusalem, which was called because Paul had made many Gentile converts.

So the question is: Do the Gentiles have to be circumcised and keep the law of Moses? At the Council, Peter, who spoke first, said they need not; he cited his own experience with the Gentile Cornelius, who received the Spirit without keeping the law. Peter said of the Gentiles that God "cleansed their hearts by faith," not by law. (This is precisely St. Paul's own great theme. For example, see Galatians 3:2.)

Then Paul and Barnabas told how they had converted Gentiles, who received the Spirit without keeping the law. (They knew that they had received the Spirit because of the miraculous gifts they were given. Hence Paul's appeal, in Galatians 3:2, to that fact as a proof.) After that James spoke, in agreement with Peter and Paul. Finally, the Council wrote to the churches of Syria and Cilicia—not to the whole world—that they need not keep the law but, as a sop to the feelings of Jews, asked them (Acts 15:29) to "abstain from what has been sacrificed to idols and from blood and from what is strangled and from unchastity."

Paul, in Galatians 2:1-10, telling of the same meeting, says that he compared notes with the Apostles and that they "added nothing to me." Paul means that they agreed on basic Christian doctrine. There was no need to mention the four concessions to Jewish feelings (one of which, avoiding unchastity, was merely general moral law) to the Galatians. The letter of the Council was addressed just to Syria and Cilicia, which did not include Galatia. The *basic doctrinal principle*, no obligation of the law for Gentiles, Paul taught everywhere with much insistence. Paul did mention the four points where they applied (see Acts 16:4). Acts also shows Paul preaching salvation by faith (see 13:39; 16:30; 20-21).

Mattill also reports on page 92 this charge: "In Acts, Paul preaches the childlike milk of a non-sacramental Jewish Christianity calling men to repent, to be baptized, to believe Jesus has risen and to await His return, whereas the genuine Paul put a curse upon anyone who should preach such a Gospel (Gal. 1:6-9)."

What Paul curses in Galatians 1:6-9 is the preaching of a Gospel that is different from what they have received. What is the basic teaching of Galatians and of Paul everywhere? Salvation by faith. But in Acts, Paul preaches that too (see 13:39; 16:30; and 20-21)—not to mention Acts 15, in which, as we saw, Paul takes part in the Council of Jerusalem giving such a teaching.

In both Acts and the Epistles, Paul does baptize (see 1 Corinthians 1:14-17). He also makes baptism basic in Romans 6:4, Ephesians 4:5, and Colossians 2:12. And if Paul preaches the Resurrection in Acts, so does he in the Epistles. First Corinthians 15, for example, is almost entirely on that subject. Again Romans 6:3-8 gives the basic principle that we die with Christ, are buried with Him (in baptism), and rise with Him. As to awaiting the return of Jesus, the same objectors like to claim that Paul expected the return of Jesus in his own lifetime. They base their argument chiefly on the words "we who are alive" in Thessalonians 4:15 and 17. Really Paul is speaking there the way teachers often speak when they say "I" or "we" to make a matter more concrete. (On awaiting the return of Jesus, see also 1 Corinthians 15:23 and 1 Thessalonians 2:19; 3:13; 4:15; 5:23.)

The same objection is based on the assumption that it is only in Acts that Paul teaches the need of repentance. The objectors have not noticed passages such as Romans 2:4, "Do you not know that God's kindness is meant to lead you to repentance?" and 2 Corinthians 7:9-10, in which Paul says he rejoices, "not because you were grieved, but because you were grieved into repenting.   .   .   . For godly grief produces a repentance that leads to salvation.   .   .   ." And in 1 Corinthians 5:3-5, Paul even hands over a sinner to Satan to bring him to repentance. (Something similar happens in 1 Timothy 1:20.)

On page 94, Mattill gives a long quote from Juelicher, saying that Paul's going through the Nazarite ceremony in Jerusalem at the suggestion of James (Acts 21:20-26) is incredible, is hypocrisy, and so, "all trust in an intelligent transmission of actual history in the Primitive Church sinks to nothing." But, really, for Paul to do that was not hypocrisy. Paul was following his own principle of 1 Corinthians 9:20-22, in which Paul gives as his *standing policy* that he becomes all things to all men. "To the Jews," says Paul, "I became as a Jew, in order to win Jews; to those under the law, I became as one under the law.   .   .   ."

There was nothing wrong with the rite in itself. It would have been wrong if Paul meant to *earn* salvation in this way. His frequent claims that we are free from the law mean only that we cannot *earn* salvation, though we can earn punishment (see Romans 6:23). Hence, though we are free from law, yet if we violate it, we are lost and will not "inherit" the kingdom. The word *inherit* implies that we do not earn salvation: Galatians 5:19-21; 1 Corinthians 6:9-10; Ephesians 5:5. See also Romans 2:6. A student speaking of salvation according to Paul put it aptly, "You can't earn it, but you can blow it." Compare also the fact that Paul carried out a vow at Cenchrae (Acts 18:18).

Mattill, also on page 94, cites this objection: "Since miracles are impossible and incredible, the accounts in Acts are either legendary or free compositions (inventions . . .). The religious dialectician of the Epistles who battles only with words, who accomplishes his work through sufferings and temptations, and who boasts only in his weakness, is supplanted in Acts by the miracle worker and magician who blinds his opponents and heals at a distance through handkerchiefs which had been in contact with his body: Paul in Acts no longer lives in the sphere of the cross but of glory."

Note first, the utterly silly prejudice that there are no miracles. Recall, however, the numerous miracles at Lourdes, all checked to the hilt by scientists. Consider the cure of Madam Biré, who had atrophy of the papilla but was made to see while the nerve was still withered. Or take the eighth-century Host of Lanciano, which turned in part to human heart muscle, while the wine turned to clots of blood—all of which were verified by a medical and biological team in 1970.[1]

Further, Paul in the Epistles does not act like a dialectician skilled with words. In 1 Corinthians 2:4-5, he says, "my speech and my message were not in plausible words of wisdom, but in demonstration of the Spirit and power, that your faith might not rest in the wisdom of men, but in the power of God." Paul means charismatic-type miracles, which gifts were routine in his day (compare 1 Corinthians 12:7-11).

In Galatians 3:2, as was noted, Paul appeals to these miracles: "Let me ask you only this: Did you receive the Spirit by works of the law, or by hearing with faith?" The way they knew that they had received the Spirit was that they received those miraculous gifts. Paul wants their faith to rest on the showing of the power of God in this way, not on his mere word. Yes, Paul in the Epistles does speak of his sufferings (for example, in 2 Corinthians 11:23-29). But in Acts he goes through the sufferings mentioned in 2 Corinthians 11—many persecutions from Jews (14:2; 17:1-10), stoning at Lystra (14:19), scourging at Philippi (16:22-23), and other trials.

A further objection (Mattill, page 94): "In Acts, where Paul

109

preaches first to the Jews, he is primarily Apostle of the Jews, only secondarily Apostle of the Gentiles. . . . According to Paul, his commission from his conversion on was only to Gentiles." We reply that his mission was to cultivate primarily the territories of the Gentiles, in contrast to Palestine. In going to such lands, he could not and should not have ignored his brethren there. Similarly Peter, who had a mission to the Jews in Galatians 2:9, also preached in Antioch and Rome. Really, Peter's commission in Matthew 28:19 was to "all nations," an assignment given him by Christ. This did not conflict with the commission spoken of in Galatians 2:9.

Still another objection (page 94) says that "without violating his principles, Paul could not have approved nor executed the Decree nor remained silent about it if it had ever existed." The Decree is, of course, that of the Council of Jerusalem mentioned in Acts 15. But that Decree agreed with Paul's great emphasis that Gentiles did not have to observe the law. Paul preached this central doctrinal point everywhere.

As to the four special points of avoiding food sacrificed to idols, blood, strangled animals, and unchastity (Acts 15:29), as we said above, the last one, avoiding unchastity, was basic moral law preached by Paul everywhere. The others were disciplinary, not doctrinal. They were sops to the Jews in Cilicia and Syria. If the Vatican sends a decision to some national episcopal conference, it applies only in that territory, not everywhere. So, too, this Decree did not bind in regard to the three points outside Syria and Cilicia—though of course the doctrinal decision that the law was not necessary would, by its nature, bind everywhere. Paul did preach the three points in those regions as we see in Acts 16:4.

A major objection on page 95 asserts that "the Paul of Acts is pre-Pauline in his Christology and post-Pauline in his natural theology, concept of the Law, and eschatology. From Acts, specifically Pauline ideas are missing, as justification and the atoning power of Jesus' death. Hence, we cannot cite any of Paul's words in Acts as if they were Paul's own."

About Christology, Paul, at Damascus right after his conversion, taught about Jesus: "He is the Son of God" (Acts 9:20). A concordance (under the word *Lord*) reveals numerous cases where Paul speaks of Jesus as "Lord," which would mean divinity to his Gentile hearers as well as to Jews (for whom the Greek *kyrios*, "Lord," was the normal Septuagint translation for the Hebrew *Yahweh*). Further, we must distinguish between what Paul would say on first contact with people from

110

what he would add later. At first, Paul would gradually build up faith. Thus to Gentiles he was apt to speak of Jesus as "a man whom He [God] has appointed" to judge the world (Acts 17:31). This is similar to what we do in apologetics, first showing that Jesus was a *messenger* sent from God (see chapter 2 above). To the Jews, he tried to show Jesus was the one long promised to Israel (compare Acts 13:16-41).

On justification, Paul teaches that it is given by faith. Acts 15 teaches that, even on the lips of Peter, who says in verse 9 that God "cleansed their hearts by faith." In 16:30, the jailer at Philippi asks Paul what to do. Paul replies, "Believe in the Lord Jesus, and you shall be saved." In this instance, Paul could speak at once of Jesus as Lord. The jailer was quite convinced by the miracle that freed Paul. Similarly at Miletus (Acts 20:21), Paul says he had been "testifying both to Jews and to Greeks of repentance to God and of faith in our Lord Jesus Christ." Now if one is saved by belief in Jesus, it is implied that Jesus does save. In Acts 17:3, Paul explains and proves "that it was necessary for the Christ to suffer and rise from the dead." Thus did Jesus atone.

As to the law, we have already shown above that Paul taught that keeping it neither merited nor earned salvation, yet violating it could earn punishment.

Finally, in regard to eschatology, it cannot be proved that Paul ever held or taught that the end was near. As we said above, his words about "we who are alive," in 1 Thessalonians 4:15 and 17, need not at all imply that he expected to see the end himself.

One final objection (Mattill, page 95): "The Paul whose speech was 'contemptible' (2 Cor. 10:10) has been transformed by Luke into an eloquent orator."

It should be noted that the charge of contemptible speech is quoted by Paul from his enemies. We need not believe them. Paul at times could be highly literary, as in the beautiful passage on love in 1 Corinthians 13. Luke, being an educated Greek, would follow Greek ways in writing history. The classic Greek historians insisted on trying to get at the facts and on adding interpretations.[2] In their speeches, pagan Greeks would always try to get the content right, but they would clothe it in their own words. Now Luke, being a companion of Paul, as can be seen from the ancient testimonies cited early in this chapter, would have ample opportunity to get the content right. Further, Paul, like most traveling speakers, would often reuse the same matter in different places. So

Luke could quite easily write up speeches fully with Paul's content—adding perhaps a bit of Lukan eloquence, according to normal Greek historiographical patterns.

This long review of objections is worthwhile because it shows us how the historical critics operate, letting us see that the arguments they use are almost always inconclusive and surely not, in this case, such as to overrule the testimony of external evidence that the author of Acts was Luke, a companion of St. Paul. Paul himself, in Philemon 24, adds greetings from "Mark, Aristarchus, Demas, and Luke, my fellow workers." In Colossians 4:14, one may read, "Luke the beloved physician and Demas greet you." And 2 Timothy 4:11 says, "Luke alone is with me." We know that it was common in ancient times to use a famous name as a pen name, but Luke was not a famous name.

All research requires, first, the gathering of all possible relevant data and, second, the use of good judgment in interpreting it. Many do well in gathering data but show poor judgment in interpreting that information. The historical critics, as was said in chapter 16, are specially prone to such bad judgment, thinking inconclusive internal evidence is conclusive. Then they build one inconclusive case on another. Today many of them, finally realizing the nature of their evidence, are showing bad judgment a second time by completely discarding the method, which is quite good if used with awareness of its limitations.

If the critics had learned from Vatican II that Scripture does not contradict Scripture, they could have saved themselves—and us—a lot of work.

Chapter 19

New Testament Source Criticism

Source criticism studies the sources used by the inspired writers. We saw in chapter 3 the chief instance of that in Old Testament source criticism, namely, the theory of the documents in the Pentateuch, the first five books of the Old Testament. We saw that Pope John Paul II, in a series of audiences, spoke favorably of the documentary theory without meaning to impose it on the Church.

The question of who is the author of an inspired book is not a question of faith but of history. Even if the sacred text itself identifies the author, we know, thanks to the genre principles, that we need not take it at face value. People then, not only used pen names, but often picked the names of famous persons. (Incidentally, this is a good reason for thinking that Luke and Mark wrote Luke and Mark. They were not famous enough that people would be likely to use their names as pen names.)

We saw too that the Technion study in Israel gives impressive evidence against the documentary theory. Quite a few scholars today are rejecting it. Some do so in the unsupported belief that the traditional data in Genesis is neither reliable nor much older than about 1500 B.C. (Abraham, Isaac, and Jacob lived well before that date.) Others reject the documentary theory because the reasons given in support of it are not at all conclusive.[1]

But now we are concerned with source criticism of the New Testament. By far the most important part of it is the Synoptic problem, since the most common solution to it, the two-source theory, is used as a major basis in form criticism of the New Testament.

What sources were used by Matthew, Mark, and Luke? The problem is fascinating because of extensive agreements in wording and sequence of events—and also because of extensive disagreements.

Out of 661 verses in Mark, about 600 are substantially found also in Matthew, and about 350 in Luke. Further, Matthew and Luke have about 236 verses in common that are not found in Mark. Yet Matthew has about 330 verses that are not found in the other two.

To put it another way, we would speak of the triple or the double tradition. The triple consists of those parts common to all three, Matthew, Mark, and Luke; the double has those found in Matthew and Luke but not in Mark. The triple tradition is found in 330 verses out of 661 in Mark; in 330 out of 1,068 in Matthew; and in 330 out of 1,150 in Luke. The double tradition appears in 230 verses of Matthew and Luke.

Further, each of the three Gospels has verses special to itself (sometimes called simple tradition). Mark has 50 of these; Matthew has over 315; while Luke has over 500 special to himself.

We notice, too, that the three Gospels have the same order of events in many places, but not in all places: Matthew and Luke have the same sequence only when they both agree with Mark.

There are also claims, somewhat exaggerated, of very closely similar wording among the Synoptics. And there are "doublets," instances in which a Gospel gives the same saying twice, indicating copying from two sources. Clearly, we do have a problem explaining both the similarities and the differences.

A key question concerns the order in which the three Synoptics were written. Eusebius of Caesarea, the first Church historian, reports (*History* 6.14.5) that Clement of Alexandria, writing around 200 A.D., said that the Gospels with genealogies (Matthew and Luke) were written before the Gospels without genealogies (Mark and John). However, Eusebius is citing a lost work purported to be by Clement, the *Hypotyposeis*, a work under suspicion of serious errors so untypical of Clement that one may wonder if the work was really by him. St. Augustine, writing two centuries later, around 400 A.D., in his *De consensu Evangelistarum* 1.2-3, thought the sequence was Matthew, Mark, Luke. Augustine added that he thought Mark epitomized Matthew. This second point—not his view on the order of composition—clashes with what Eusebius (*History* 3.39.15) also tells us Papias wrote, that Mark was the interpreter of Peter's preaching and, so, would not be summarizing Matthew. Papias, however, says nothing on the order of composition of the three Synoptics. Papias himself was very early. St. Irenaeus (*Against Heresies* 5.33.4), writing around 200 A.D., says that Papias was a companion of St. Polycarp, who had known the Apostle St. John personally. Irenaeus also gives the sequence as Matthew, Mark, Luke. The Muratorian Canon, dating probably from 170-190 A.D., explicitly makes Luke the third Gospel—though the first lines, which would have spoken of Matthew and Mark, are lost.

The testimony of early writers, then, does definitely say that the order is Matthew, Mark, and Luke. It should be noted that these witnesses seem to speak of the original Hebrew text of Matthew, which is lost, rather than of our present Greek text, whose sequence might be different.

Pope Leo XIII, in his *Providentissimus Deus*, 1893, made a valuable observation. "Unfortunately," said Leo, "and with damage to religion, there has arisen a method, dignified by the name of higher criticism, in which the origin, integrity, and authority of each book [of Scripture] is judged by only internal reasons. On the contrary it is clear that in questions of history, such as the origin and transmission of books, the testimonies of history have more weight than other things, and that these testimonies should be sought out and examined as studiously as possible; but that the internal reasons are in general not of such weight that they should be used except for a confirmatory argument."

When Leo XIII wrote these words, they would have met with a cold reception. But today, when many prominent scholars are attacking the historical-critical method, and seeing that its almost exclusive reliance on internal evidence has led to inconclusive results today, his words are coming true. We need to keep them in mind, especially in examining the Synoptic problem.

Numerous solutions to the problem have been proposed. For our purpose, we can reduce the choices to a few general types. Proponents of the oral-catechesis theory think that teaching on the words and deeds of Jesus was given in a more or less fixed, stereotyped form, both in Aramaic and in Greek. Matthew would represent the form current in Palestine; Mark, that in Rome; Luke, the form at Antioch or in the Pauline churches. This theory has not met with much favor. It makes the Evangelists mere recorders rather than real authors. One serious weakness of this theory is that it cannot account for the fact that some things—the Our Father and the words of institution of the Eucharist, for example—are found in varied forms.

Another theory proposes mutual dependence of the Evangelists. The simplest form of this theory says that one Gospel is the source of the others, or that two are the source of the third. Few hold this simple view today.

A more refined view says that an Aramaic or Hebrew Matthew came first and that various complete or incomplete Greek translations were made from it. Meanwhile, oral tradition was evolving. Then Mark used one of these translations plus the preaching of Peter at Rome. Luke used Mark and also a Greek version of Matthew.

A variation on this theme is the theory that Luke used Matthew and that Mark used both Matthew and Luke. This was first proposed in 1764 by an Englishman named Owen. It is better known from the work of J. Griesbach, in 1783, which today is strongly defended by William R. Farmer (*The Synoptic Problem*, Western North Carolina Press, 1976, and Hans-Herbert Stoldt, *History and Criticism of the Markan Hypothesis*, tr. D. L. Niewyk, Mercer University Press, 1980). This theory would explain both the triple and the double tradition. The special agreements of Matthew and Luke would stem from Luke's use of Matthew. The similarity of order between Matthew and Mark would come from Mark's following of the outline of Matthew except at times where Mark chose to follow Luke. The chief difficulty is to explain why Mark would have omitted so much material from his sources. There is also an objection concerning the sequence of incidents: the Gospels of Matthew and Luke agree in order only when they both also agree with Mark.

That Mark wrote first is almost universally accepted today as is the dependence of Luke on Mark. Less generally accepted, but still widely held, is the view that Matthew depends on Mark. Some dispute this last point strongly, insisting that Matthew came first.

The third type of solution is the two-source theory. According to it, Mark wrote first, using oral tradition. But at almost the same time there arose a sayings source called Q (for German *Quelle*, "source"). Many think this Q had only sayings, no narrative matter, and add that this is the Logia, or sayings of Jesus, which Papias spoke of as written by Matthew. Much agreement in wording in the discourse material common to Matthew and Luke is said to support the existence of Q, as does the presence of doublets, sayings given twice in a Gospel. One would have come from Mark, one from Q.

We cannot offer a definitive solution—no one can. But some things can be said. There really are remarkable similarities in wording, but the wording is not identical in many instances. The best way to see this for oneself is to make point-by-point, word-by-word comparisons between parallel passages in the Gospels. To be fair, we might suggest an incident in which the similarities are specially strong. An example of this is the healing of a leper as reported in Matthew 8:2-4, Mark 1:40-45, and Luke 5:12-16. By far the easiest way to study these texts is to get a volume that prints the four Gospels in parallel columns. One of the best is by Kurt Aland, *Synopsis Quattuor Evangeliorum*, Stuttgart, 1978. This has the texts in Greek. There is also an English edition, *Synopsis of the Four Gospels, Greek-English Edition* of *Synopsis Quattuor Evangeliorum*, United Bible Societies 1979.

The case of the so-called doublets is not as clear as some claim. For example, in chapter 9 of his Gospel, Luke reports a trial mission of *the twelve*; at the start of chapter 10, he reports: "After this the Lord appointed *seventy others*, and sent them on ahead of him . . ." (emphasis added). Clearly we could have, not a pure duplication, but two different incidents. As a traveling speaker, Jesus would be very apt to say the same thing in more than one place, with some variations. (A convenient list of "doublets" is found in Stoldt, cited above, on pp. 174-175). So this argument is not really convincing, yet many consider it a chief proof of the two-source theory.

One of the more telling arguments against that theory is the presence of the so-called minor agreements of Matthew and Luke against Mark. In some passages in which all three Synoptics report the same incident, there are significant agreements, yet Matthew and Luke agree in differing from Mark in small points. For example, in Matthew 21:1-9 and Luke 19:28-37, there are seventeen points in which these two agree in disagreeing with Mark 11:1-10.[2] The point is, how can Matthew and Luke unite against Mark on these details if they both followed Mark, as the two-source theory claims?

In addition to the problem of the minor agreements just mentioned, there is impressive evidence against Marcan priority.

My article "Did St. Luke Imitate the Septuagint?" (*Journal for the Study of the New Testament*, vol. 15, 1982, pp. 30-41) presents numerous cases in which Luke employs a very odd Semitic structure that in no case at all is found in the parallel passages in Mark (see our chapter 12). So, if Luke copied Mark, why would he have added Semitisms that Mark, a native Semite, did not use? Similarly, as H. F. D. Sparks says, Luke's Gospel is notable for a "continual rephrasing of St. Mark: in order to add Semitisms."[3] An example is found in the parable of the wicked husbandmen. In Mark's version (12:1-12), we find that after the first failure, the master "sent another slave." Still later, "he sent another." Luke's version (20:9-19) says, "And he *added* to send another servant. . . . And he *added* to send a third" (emphases added). This is a pure Hebrew idiom, *ysf*. On the other hand, in a few places Mark has Hebraisms that Luke does *not* copy (Mark 6:39 and 8:12), even though everyone concedes that Luke is more inclined to Semitisms than Mark (see our discussion of this in chapter 12).

As M. Zerwick shows,[4] Luke often uses an Aramaic pattern of a form of the verb *to be* plus a participle instead of an imperfect indicative. Luke has fifty percent of all such cases in the entire New Testament—thirty examples in his Gospel and twenty-four in Acts of the Apostles. Yet, where Mark *does* have this structure, Luke usually avoids it, though he uses it in places that are parallel to Mark but in which Mark *does not* have it.

In regard to adding or omitting details, a study by Leslie R. Keylock[5] shows that Luke is more detailed than Mark forty-seven times, less so thirty-seven times; while Matthew is more precise than Mark fifty-eight times, less so fifty-four times. In all, there is quite a bit of impressive evidence against Marcan priority.

What does the Church say of the Synoptic problem? The Pontifical Biblical Commission, on June 26, 1912, after insisting on the Matthew-Mark-Luke sequence and the early dates for each, said that scholars are free to appeal to theories of oral or written tradition, or to the dependence of one Gospel on another, yet those scholars should "not easily embrace" the two-source theory. This judgment by the Commission led to a revision of the theory by many Catholic scholars, yet, substantially, it is still defended by very many. Interestingly, the 1964 Instruction of the same Commission, "On the Historical Truth of the Gospel," did not mention the theory. Nor did Vatican II comment. The Commission's Instruction will be examined in detail in the following chapters.

Our conclusion? We have a problem that is likely to remain unsolved until new evidence is developed. Yet it has been worthwhile to examine it for anyone who wants to know what is going on in Scripture studies today, since it is basic to form and redaction criticism, and since so many scholars dogmatically persist in the erroneous judgment that Mark wrote first.

Chapter 20

Prejudices of Form and Redaction Critics

Many today are overawed at the technical and recondite nature of the new methods of Scripture study. No one trained before these methods were developed can know anything about Scripture, they suppose. Form and redaction criticism are the most awe-inspiring part of this picture. But really, there is nothing too difficult to understand here. To make this clear, we will begin by giving a brief presentation of form and redaction criticism, treating both together, since the 1964 Instruction of the Biblical Commission does that, and since, by nature, one follows the other.

There were three stages in the development of our Gospels: (1) Jesus said and did certain things; (2) the Apostles and others in the first generation preached Jesus' words and deeds; and (3) individuals within the Church, moved by the Holy Spirit, wrote down part of this basic preaching. Incidentally, it should now be easy to see how we could say at the close of chapter 15 that the Church has something more basic than Scripture. The Gospels are simply part of her own basic teaching, set down under inspiration. In this sense, too, one can speak of only one source of revelation.

To find out at which of these three stages a given item in the Gospels took its present form, and to learn something about it, our first task is to classify each part according to its literary form. For almost any passage in the Gospels, the critics think, could be made up of several of these units, especially since people in stage 2 were apt to report at one time just one unit: one saying of Jesus, or one thing Jesus did. Some of these forms are apt to contain more fact than others, just as various genres assert different things.

In this connection, we should try to determine the life-setting, what the Germans call the *Sitz-im-Leben*, of a unit. Different life situations are apt to call for the use of different forms, and vice versa.

Next—and now comes an unfortunate development—we try to see which things can be trusted, for very many critics have thought that the Christian community was "creative," that is, apt to just fake things.

To do this, certain criteria must be used. Chiefly there are four of them: (1) DOUBLE DISSIMILARITY OR IRREDUCIBILITY: if an idea is dissimilar to the emphases of both ancient Judaism and early Christianity, we may think it comes from Jesus Himself; (2) MULTIPLE ATTESTATION: if we find the same idea in different literary forms, it is more likely to be genuine; (3) COHERENCE: an item is apt to be authentic if it is consistent with material that we already know is authentic by other criteria; (4) LINGUISTIC AND ENVIRONMENTAL TESTS: if the material does not fit with the languages spoken or the environment of the ministry of Jesus, we reject it. That it does fit, however, is not enough to prove that it is authentic.

Many critics, notably Rudolf Bultmann, the father of New Testament form criticism, think there is little we can be sure of about Jesus. He believes that there is a gap between the Jesus of history (what He really was) and the Christ of faith (what the Church preaches about Him). Bultmann wanted to get around the gap by making the Gospels mean the same as the bizarre existentialism of Heidegger. (Fully developed liberation theology uses Marxism in the same way.)

The study of the first two phases (the words and acts of Jesus, plus the preaching of the early Church) is called form criticism; the study of the work of the Evangelists in handling this material is called redaction criticism.

The only thing hard to understand about this type of criticism is the remarkable dullness of some of the prejudices the critics bring to the task. For in the above outline, certain assumptions are apparent. The notion of "the creative community," for example. To examine this line of criticism in more detail, we will follow the Instruction on the Historical Truth of the Gospels, from the Pontifical Biblical Commission of April 21, 1964. The Latin text, plus an English translation, can be found in *Catholic Biblical Quarterly*, vol. 26 (July 1964), on pp. 299-304 for the Latin, and pp. 305-312 for the English. (We will, however, make our own translation here.)

On the very first page, the Instruction calls for scholars to work hard because "the truth of the actions and words contained in the Gospels is being challenged." The Instruction calls on the exegete "to work hard to open up the true sense of the Scriptures, relying not only on his own ability but especially trusting firmly in the help of God and the light of the Church." To this end, the Instruction insists on five points.

First, the exegete should make use of the work of previous scholars, especially the holy Fathers and Doctors of the Church. (Many scholars glide lightly over this point.) He should "diligently employ the new helps to exegesis, especially those which the historical method, taken broadly, provides. This method diligently seeks out the sources and their nature and force, and gathers the helps given by textual criticism, literary criticism, and a knowledge of languages. The exegete will observe the admonition of Pius XII . . . 'to prudently . . . seek out how the form of expression or the literary genre employed by the sacred writer helps towards true and genuine understanding'. . . . Finally the exegete will use all means by which he may see more deeply the nature of the testimony of the Gospels."

After these introductory things, the Instruction adds the following: "Where the situation calls for it, the exegete is permitted to investigate what sound elements there are in the 'method of the history of forms,' which he can use for a fuller understanding of the Gospels."

Evidently there is good to be had from form and redaction criticism. Note, however, that the Instruction merely says that its use is "permitted." It does not say that it must be done. Further, it warns: "But let him yet be circumspect, for there are often joined to this method unacceptable philosophical and theological principles which not rarely vitiate the method itself and its conclusions on literary matters."

We often hear this Instruction cited as an unqualified go-ahead for scholars to use these methods. Yes, there is a green light, but there are many warnings as well. To ignore them leads to great distortion.

Here are the unacceptable principles: "Certain followers of this method, led astray by the prejudices of rationalism, [1] reject the existence of a supernatural order and the intervention of a personal God in the world as taught by revelation properly so called and [2] the possibility and actual existence of miracles and prophecies. [3] Others start with a false notion of faith, as if faith does not care about historical truth or is even incompatible with it. [4] Others deny, as it were in advance, the historical value and character of the documents of revelation. [5] Others, finally, think little of the authority of the Apostles as witnesses of Christ, and of their role and influence on the primitive community, while they extol the creative power of this community. All these things are not only opposed to Catholic doctrine but also lack a scientific foundation, and are foreign to the right principles of the historical method." (Numbers have been inserted in the text for convenience in discussion.)

There is no need to use much space to prove that unbelievers and some Protestants hold such prejudices. A few samples will suffice. R. Bultmann says that today "nobody reckons with direct intervention by transcendent powers" (*Jesus Christ and Mythology*, Charles Scribner's Sons, N.Y., 1958, p. 36). On page 15 of that book, Bultmann writes: "The whole conception of the world which is presupposed in the preaching of Jesus as in the New Testament generally is mythological . . . the conception of the intervention of supernatural powers in the course of events; and the conception of miracles. . . . We call [it] mythological because it is different from the conception of the world which has been formed and developed by science. . . . Modern science does not believe that the course of nature can be interrupted." Patrick Henry, in his broad survey *New Directions in New Testament Study* (Westminster, 1979, pp. 252-253), reports various views: "Much more important is the Bible's own portrayal of the 'piety of doubt' the 'faithfulness of uncertainty.' Even Paul said that 'now we see in a mirror dimly' . . . and that *now* is the time of pilgrimage. . . . Paul also insists that we do not have certain knowledge of things to come. . . . Interpretations of the New Testament which make of revelation either the direct voice of God or the mystery veiled by the language are simply not serviceable for persons on pilgrimage."

Some Catholics make unfortunate statements on item 1 above, revelation. Thus the noted catechetical specialist Gabriel Moran, with Sr. Maria Harris, in "Revelation and Religious" (*National Catholic Reporter*, November 22, 1967, p. 6), wrote of *revelation* as denoting a "present happening." Moran and Harris say that "it is impossible to come to a present, personal, social revelation by building upon a thing that is handed down from the past. . . . The only way that God does not speak is in generalities to the general mass."

About the possibility and actuality of miracles (item 2) there is extensive trimming on the Catholic side. R. Brown reports that to accept all Gospel miracles would be fundamentalism, and says no respectable scholar, Catholic or Protestant, today follows such an approach. It would make New Testament times a kind of fairyland. The more conservative scholars, he says, accept some miracles, e.g., the virginal conception and the resurrection, but they do not believe in possession by devils.[1]

Brown himself makes some puzzling statements about the virginal conception. On the one hand, he says it is "lucidly clear" that Matthew believed in it.[2] Yet since he cannot trace it by identifiable witnesses, he says it leaves an unresolved problem.[3] Of course, he is assuming we cannot suppose testimony came from His Mother Mary. But Pope John Paul II, in a General Audience of January 18, 1988, said something that is obvious: "To identify the source of the infancy narrative one must go back to St. Luke's remark: 'Mary kept all these things, pondering them in her heart.' . . . Mary . . . could bear witness, after Christ's death and resurrection, in regard to what concerned herself and her role as Mother, precisely in the apostolic period when the New Testament texts were being written."

As to the resurrection of Jesus, James Mackey asserts, "We have in the New Testament no evidence offered us which was ever of an objectively verifiable kind and which could prove the personal resurrection of Jesus."[4] Mackey seems to want us to simply believe. He says that it is just "the experience" of the power of Jesus in our lives, that "can alone convince us today that Jesus lives and reigns."

About demons, Brown makes a strange statement that the New Testament shows us Jesus and Paul were serious about the demonic world. But Brown himself wrote, "I do not believe that demons inhabit desert places or the upper air, as Jesus and Paul thought. . . . I see no way to get around the difficulty except by saying that Jesus and Paul were wrong on this point. They accepted the beliefs of their times about demons, but those beliefs were superstitious."[5] So the incarnate Son of God harbored even some superstitions!

Such a claim overlooks two things. First, when Jesus spoke of a demon going to a desert place (Matthew 12:43-45), He was giving a sort of parable, as we can see from the concluding line: "So also it will be with this wicked generation." He meant that He came and broke the power of Satan over the Jews. They will reject Him and fall back worse than before. So the text does not mean Jesus believed demons live in the desert. As to St. Paul, he did speak in Ephesians 2:2 of "the aeon of this world, according to the ruler of the power of the air." But he was using the language of his opponents to counter them—not expressing his own belief in a place for demons. For in Colossians and also in Ephesians Paul was working against views of either the Gnostics or of Jewish apocalyptic speculators that spoke of such aeons, whom we should, according to them, worship along with Christ.

This charge of superstition is part of a larger picture. It is epidemic today to charge Jesus with much ignorance: He did not know He was Messiah or divine. He was ignorant of many other things. For documentation on who has said what, and the answer to them, see W. Most, *The Consciousness of Christ.*

Of course, we see attempts to explain away many miracles. Thus J. Fitzmyer wrote that today, anyone who reads Mark 9:14-29 and Matthew 17:15 can see that the boy from whom Jesus drove out an evil spirit was epileptic. Fitzmyer comments: "Undoubtedly, Jesus shared some of the protological thinking [of the times] himself, being a child of his time."[6] If the boy really was epileptic—how can we be sure?—Jesus would have known that fact, but need not have explained to the people of His time. His mission was not to give medical information.

Many today also devalue the Old Testament Messianic prophecies, saying we can get something out of them only by hindsight. But a study of the Targums, ancient Jewish Aramaic translations plus fill-ins on Scripture, shows they understood very much indeed. As to their date—no matter what the date—they were made without seeing them fulfilled in Jesus, whom they hated. Further, Jacob Neusner, one of the best Jewish scholars today, in his exhaustive study, *Messiah in Context,*[7] reviews all Jewish writings from after the fall of Jerusalem to the Babylonian Talmud (completed 500-600 A.D.). Before that Talmud, the Jews showed scant interest in the Messianic prophecies. In the Talmud they do get interested, but the only point of the classic prophecies they mention is that the Messiah was to be of the line of David. How then could the parts of the Targums that go into such detail on the Messiah have been written in an age when the Jews had hardly any interest in the prophecies?

About the third item, an unfortunate concept of faith, we can recall the views, discussed in chapter 6, of Thomas Hoffman, who wants faith to lack a rational foundation. This is much the same idea as is found in "the leap" of Kierkegaard and Bultmann. Sadly the ideas of Hoffman are diffused on a popular level in *The New Guide in Reading and Studying the Bible*, by Wilfrid Harrington (Wilmington, Del., revised 1984, pp. 25-28). This book summarizes and explicitly refers to Hoffman's article.

As to items 4 and 5, some Catholic authors do have little confidence in the historical value of the Gospels, as we shall see in the next chapters. The Biblical Commission had ample reason for its warnings. We may and should make use of the resources of form and redaction criticism, but we must be alert for the dangers mentioned.

Chapter 21

Form and Redaction Criticism

I

Right after giving the warnings we saw in chapter 20, the Biblical Commission Instruction of 1964 begins to explain the three stages in the development of the Gospels.

The first stage consists of the words and actions of Jesus Himself: "Christ the Lord joined disciples to Himself, who followed Him from the beginning and saw His works and heard His words, and in this way were suited to be witnesses of His life and teaching."

Thus, the testimony of the Gospels goes back to eyewitnesses who had seen and heard everything from the beginning. Moreover, Jesus Himself, in presenting His teaching, quite naturally did what any good speaker would do. He adapted His presentation to His audience: "The Lord, when He was orally giving His doctrine, followed the ways of reasoning and presentation that were usual in His time; in this way He accommodated Himself to the mentality of His hearers, and saw to it that what He taught would be firmly impressed on their minds, and would be easily retained in memory by the disciples. They correctly understood the miracles in such a way that through them men might believe in Christ and accept in faith the doctrine of salvation."

Some scholars today, even some Catholics, try to say that Jesus never intended His miracles to prove anything. They were "just signs," these scholars say. But it makes sense to ask what they were signs of.

The real answer is that they were evidence of His mission and power. Hence, over and over again, He called on people whom He healed to have faith. In context, He was calling them to have faith in His power and mission.

In the second stage of the formation of the Gospels, according to the Biblical Commission Instruction of 1964, "the Apostles proclaimed chiefly the death and resurrection of the Lord, and faithfully presented His life and words, taking into account in their manner of preaching the circumstances of their hearers."

This is what Jesus Himself had done, for He too adjusted His presentation to His audience. So we can begin to see that while the Apostles might use different words than our Lord did in preaching His message, they did it without changing the sense, for "they faithfully presented His life and words."

We are here far from the imaginings of some critics who think the early community was "creative"—that Jesus' followers just made up things so that in a debate between two factions in the community, if the people in faction A did not have a saying of Jesus to support their position, they would make one up, and faction B would counter with the same creativity. This is impossible because the Apostles were in control. There were no headless groups, each running its own way. Acts 5:12-13 tells us that "many signs and wonders were done among the people by the hands of the Apostles. And they were all together in Solomon's Portico. None of the rest dared join them, but the people held them in high honor." The people knew that the Apostles, as the Instruction said, "followed Him from the beginning and saw His works and heard His words, and in this way were suited to be witnesses to His life and teaching."

Another argument against the existence of a freewheeling "creative" community was the simple fact that all knew their eternity depended on getting the facts about Jesus and His teaching. As St. Paul, in 1 Corinthians 15:17-18, told the faithful: "If Christ has not been raised, your faith is futile and you are still in your sins. Then those also who have fallen asleep in Christ have perished."

What the critics call creativity was all the stronger, according to them, because it had so long a time to operate, for the Gospels were late in being written. Mark, they commonly think, was a little before 70 A.D. Matthew and Luke they assign to the period 80-90 A.D. The evidence offered for these late dates consists of indications found within the Gospel. For example, the clarity of Luke on the prophecy of the fall of Jerusalem, these critics say, shows that it was written *after* the event. But the strong testimony of early writers, external evidence, shows otherwise. And even if the Gospels were as late as 80-90 A.D., the first apologist, Quadratus, writing about 123 A.D., tells us that in his day people were still alive who had been healed or raised from the dead by Jesus. That need not mean 123 A.D., but it surely covers the later period 80-90 A.D.

As to the changes of wording and adaptation to their audience, the Instruction tells us that the Apostles would benefit in their preaching from the fuller light they enjoyed after Easter and Pentecost: "After Jesus rose from the dead and His divinity was clearly seen, the faith [of the Apostles], far from destroying the memory of the things that had happened, instead strengthened it, because their faith rested on the things which Jesus had done and taught."

If we wonder how their faith could have destroyed the memory of what Jesus said and did, the answer is that the Instruction has in mind those who think the Apostles first idealized Jesus, then divinized Him, and so lost sight of what He really had said and done.

The Instruction does not say that His divinity was *more* clearly seen after the Resurrection. It merely says when it was *"clearly* seen." So the Instruction does not tell us whether or not the Apostles understood His divinity at all before the Resurrection. What of the fact that Jesus, in reply to Peter's confession that He was "the Christ, the Son of the living God" (Matthew 16:16-17), said: "Blessed are you, Simon Bar-Jona! For flesh and blood has not revealed this to you, but my Father who is in heaven"? Does the fact that Jesus said Peter had had a revelation have to mean that the revelation said Jesus was divine? Not necessarily. It could have meant Peter received a correct understanding of Messiahship, in contrast to the false notions then current. Or it could have been some dim notion of the divinity of Jesus, which would become clearer later on. Either possibility would fit with the words of the Instruction. (The words "Son of God" could be applied at that time to any devout Jew. See Hosea 11:1.)

It could be objected that if Peter had known of Jesus' divinity, he could not have denied Him later. But Peter might have learned by means of an interior locution. Such revelations are clear when first given, but can later fade, as we learn from a Doctor of the Church who had experienced them, St. Teresa of Avila (*Interior Castle*, 6.3).

131

Next the Instruction follows up on the question of whether faith could destroy or distort the memory of the Person of Jesus and what He said. "The worship which the disciples thereafter extended to Jesus as Lord and Son of God did not change Him into a 'mythical person,' nor was His doctrine deformed." As was noted briefly above, it was Rudolf Bultmann and his school who held that there is a gap between the Jesus of history (what He really was) and the Christ of faith (what the Apostles later preached). This gap happened, they claim, precisely because of the idealization that took place, plus the creativity of the community.

How to answer these critics? The claim rests on subjectivity, not on hard, firm evidence. It is the recognition of this subjectivity that is today leading many prominent critics to abandon form criticism altogether. It should be noted, too, that there is a way of bridging the alleged gap, or better, of simply bypassing it: the use of the method sketched in chapter 2. There are six very simple facts about Jesus in the Gospels, things so simple that entanglement with culture and subjective dispositions could not have affected them, facts whose accurate presentation is assured by the concern of the preachers for their own eternity. Finding these six facts proves that we have on hand a group, a Church, commissioned to teach by a messenger sent from God, and promised God's protection. Then we not only intellectually may, but intellectually must, believe that group, the Church, which can tell us in a guaranteed way about the doctrine of Jesus.

The Instruction makes no mention of the four criteria, which were summarized in chapter 20, to see if something came from Jesus. They are not needed once we have gone through the six facts, for the Church assures us that on things beyond the six, the Scriptures do give us at least the substance of what Jesus said. These facts would not, of course, prevent the Apostles from using different words for the benefit of their hearers, adapting themselves to the current audience, as Jesus Himself had done. The change of wording would still preserve the sense faithfully.

The Instruction now returns to the fact that the teaching of the Apostles would have benefited from their clearer understanding after Easter and Pentecost. "However," the Instruction says, "we should not deny that the Apostles handed down to their hearers the things really said and done by the Lord in the light of that fuller understanding which they enjoyed after being taught by the glorious events of Christ and by the light of the Spirit of Truth. Thus it happened that just as Jesus

Himself after His resurrection 'interpreted to them' both the words of the Old Testament and His own words, so too they [the Apostles] interpreted His words and deeds as the needs of their hearers called for."

Over and over again the Gospels, with admirable honesty and candor, portray the Apostles as dull and slow to understand during the public life of Jesus. So the Apostles, in using that greater light, would *not* and did not paint themselves as having understood at a time when they still did not understand. No, but the Apostles would bring out their better grasp of the Old Testament prophecies and of the richness in the words of Jesus Himself.

The Church today still continues to penetrate ever deeper into the message of Jesus, as is seen from the fact that new doctrinal decisions, even definitions, have come down to us over the course of the centuries, and still come to us today. Those new teachings are not new revelations but deeper penetrations into the deposit of faith once given (see Vatican II, *On Divine Revelation*, n. 4).

Next the Instruction speaks further on this matter of adapted presentation: "Devoting themselves to the ministry of the word [see Acts 6:4], they preached, using various forms of speaking that would fit with their purpose and the mentality of the hearers; for they were under obligation [to bring the truth of salvation] 'to Greeks and to barbarians, both to the wise and to the foolish' [see Romans 1:14]. These manners of speaking in which the heralds announced Christ should be distinguished and appraised: catecheses, narratives, testimonies, hymns, doxologies, prayers and other literary forms commonly used in Sacred Scripture by men of that time."

One of the first steps in form criticism (see chapter 20) is to identify these forms[1] so as to see what the Apostles and Evangelists meant to assert. For it is only when we know the rules of the genre being employed that we will rightly judge what is asserted and what is not. However, everything that is asserted was and is true, as Vatican II tells us: "Since all that the inspired authors or sacred writers assert should be regarded as asserted by the Holy Spirit, we must acknowledge that the books of Scripture firmly, faithfully, and without error teach that truth which God, for the sake of our salvation, wished to be confided to Sacred Scripture" (*On Divine Revelation*, n. 11).

This brings us to what the Instruction has to say about stage 3, the work of the inspired authors (which is really redaction criticism). "The sacred authors entrusted this primitive instruction, first given orally, then in writing—for it soon happened that many attempted to put in order a narration of the things [see Luke 1:1] that pertained to the Lord Jesus—they entrusted it to the four Gospels for the benefit of the churches, according to the method and special purpose that each had in mind. By selecting some things from the many things handed down, by making a synthesis of certain things, by every resource they strove, keeping in mind the state of the churches, that their readers might have assurance about the words in which they had been instructed [see Luke 1:4]. For the sacred writers, out of the things handed down to them, selected chiefly those things which were suited to the various circumstances of the faithful and to the goal they had chosen."

Notice that the Evangelists used both oral and written sources. (On St. Luke's meticulous use of sources, see chapter 12.) The Gospels are really part of the original preaching set down under inspiration. The Instruction stresses that only part of the original tradition was set down in writing, for the Evangelists selected some things but did not take all. Further they synthesized some things. St. Matthew, for example, in the Sermon on the Mount, seems to have put together things said by Jesus on several occasions. This selection was guided, the Instruction notes, by two things: the special goals each Evangelist set for himself, and the particular needs of local churches for which the Evangelists wrote. For example, St. Matthew is specially intent on bringing out the fulfillment of prophecies in Jesus and in speaking of the Church. St. Luke stresses the universality, the mission to the Gentiles.

Yet not always can we determine just what the special goals were. The problem is especially difficult with Mark's Gospel. The traditional view was that he wrote at Rome, recording the preaching of St. Peter. Some still hold this view, e.g., Martin Hengel of Tubingen, in his *Studies in the Gospel of Mark* (tr. J. Bowden, Philadelphia: Fortress, 1985, p. 29). Hengel thinks the purpose was to help Christians facing Nero's persecution. Still others, e.g., Wilfred Harrington (*Mark*, p. xii), thinks it comes from a Christian community in Syria between 66 and 70 A.D. R. Brown, in *Antioch and Rome* (Brown and Meir, Paulist, 1983), simply admits we cannot know the purpose Mark had in mind and adds that we cannot really be sure we can tell what is tradition and what is Mark's editing (pp. 199-200). C. F. Evans, in *The Cambridge History of the Bible* (3 vols., Cambridge University, 1960-63 I, pp. 270-271), is almost in despair on this question about Mark.

That is quite an admission! If we cannot really be sure what is tradition and what is redaction in Mark, no wonder there is a tone of despair in the comment of C. F. Evans. We can see that there is heavy subjectivity and insecurity involved in form criticism.

Notice, finally, the stress the Instruction places on the reliability of the Evangelists. Not only are they dependent on the tradition of those who had been eyewitnesses to Jesus from the beginning, but they took great care and "by every resource they strove . . . that their readers might have assurance about the words in which they had been instructed." This is a deliberate echo, as the footnote tells us, of Luke 1:4, in which Luke says that he made a most careful investigation to assure Theophilus of the truth.

Chapter 22

Form and Redaction Criticism

II

The Instruction has told us that the Evangelists may change the wording of the reports about Jesus while faithfully keeping the sense. Now it adds that the various incidents in the life of Jesus were not always reported in the same sequence as that in which they occurred, and perhaps an item might be affected by being placed in a different context.

"Since the meaning of a statement depends also on the sequence," the Instruction says, "the Evangelists in handing on the words and deeds of the Savior explained them, one writer in one context, another in another, for the benefit of the readers. So the exegete should search out what the Evangelist meant in putting a word or deed in this way in a certain context. For the fact that the Evangelists report the words or deeds of the Lord in different order does not affect at all the truth of the narrative, for they keep the sense while reporting His statements, not to the letter, but in different ways."

If we compare the various Gospels, it is apparent that they do not always report events in the same sequence. There is apt to be some bunching, such as is commonly thought to have occurred in St. Matthew's report of the Sermon on the Mount. And there are other kinds of variations of sequence too. The Instruction tells us that mere variation in sequence in itself does not affect the truth. The reason is the writer's concern, which the Instruction has insisted on, to report accurately the information that came from those who themselves had been witnesses.

It is even possible to say that a change in sequence may result in putting a saying of Jesus in a different context. And context can affect sense. But, the sense that the Evangelist intended to express in this way is what he *asserted*, and that, as we saw in our discussion of Vatican II in chapter 21, is also *asserted* by the Holy Spirit. So we should seek out what that sense is.

Is it often that there is a real change of sense resulting from a change of context? Not really, but an interesting example is found in the Gospels of Matthew and Luke. Matthew 10:27 says, "What I tell you in the dark, utter in the light; and what you hear whispered, proclaim upon the housetops." Luke 12:2-3, however, has this: "Nothing is covered up that will not be revealed, or hidden that will not be known. Whatever you have said in the dark shall be heard in the light, and what you have whispered in private rooms shall be proclaimed upon the housetops."

The context shows that the saying in Matthew means that the Apostles will later preach in public what Jesus told them in private. That is of course true. In Luke, however, the saying refers to the hypocrisy of the Pharisees. It will come to light. And that, too, is true. Each Evangelist made use of a saying to teach a different truth. But both items were true. (We happen to know, from a Targum or Qoheleth 12:13, that the saying was a proverb.) But, and this is important, if we check the six basic facts used in chapter 2 to reestablish the teaching authority of the Church, not one of them is by nature such that it could vary in sense if placed in a different context. Hence the basic doctrine is fully safeguarded, and the shifts in sense of the type we have seen all yield truths.

St. Paul not infrequently uses Old Testament texts in a way different from their use in the original context. For example, in Romans 1:17, Paul quotes the prophet Habakkuk (2:4), "The righteous shall live by faith," to bring out his great theme of justification by faith. Yet Habakkuk was referring to something else. He meant that Judah's deliverance would be accomplished through fidelity to God, in contrast to the Chaldean invaders, who depended on their own might. Yet, this change by Paul not only did not falsify the doctrine of Christ, rather it taught it all the more clearly as a result of the guidance of the Holy Spirit, under which Paul wrote.

It is often said today that the Gospels are not "factual history." A careful study of the genre of the Gospels (see W. Most, *Catholic Apologetics Today*, chapters 8 and 10) shows that the genre of the Gospels was one in which the inspired writer wanted to recount facts, plus interpreta-

138

tions, and that the inspired writers were in a position to get the facts, and that they most intensely wanted to report them accurately, even if, as the Instruction says, they might change the sequence of the account. They believed correctly that their very eternity would depend on knowing the truth about Jesus and His teaching. For example, we know from the First Epistle of Clement I (5.1), which scholars date to c. 94 A.D., that Sts. Peter and Paul were of the same generation. This is obvious, for Peter and Paul died around 66 A.D. Clement became Pope in 92, a span of about 26 years. Clearly, one old enough to be Pope would have known them and would have firsthand data from them. Or again, St. Ignatius, eaten by the lions in Rome about 107 A.D., says in his Letter to Rome that he wanted much to die for Christ. A man facing lions will not deal in fancies about Christ!

The Instruction comments: "Since from the results of new investigations it is clear that the doctrine and life of Jesus were not merely recounted for the sole purpose of being remembered, but were 'preached' so as to provide for the Church the foundation of faith and morals, the interpreter, in unwearyingly studying the testimony of the Evangelists, will be able to bring out more profoundly the permanent theological value of the Gospels, and to show in full light how greatly necessary and important is the Church's interpretation [of the Gospels]."

The very fact that we have seen the possibilities of variations in sense that we have just described does make it all the more necessary to have a providentially protected Church that is able to give us a divinely guaranteed interpretation of the Scriptures. Yet it must be insisted that the testimony of the Gospels on the six points studied in chapter 2, which establish the teaching commission of the Church, can be had even without the interpretation of the Church. The very simple nature of the six points makes that help unnecessary and avoids the vicious circle that would result if we did depend on the Church for the six points.

In the very next paragraph, the Instruction underscores again this need of the Church. It says that the exegete "must always be ready to obey the magisterium of the Church, and must not forget that the Apostles, filled with the Holy Spirit, preached the good news and that the Gospels were written under the inspiration of the Holy Spirit, who kept their authors from all errors."

Still another difficulty is often raised today: Scripture is "time-conditioned." This is true, if we make the needed distinctions. It is true, as we said in chapter 1, that the Holy Spirit uses the human author in such a way that he retains his own characteristics of style, good or not so good. It is also true that the particular words and literary genres he uses are affected by the culture of his own land and time period.

This does not mean that we cannot find the truth even so. Differences of mere style, of course, are no problem. What of the literary genre? We have already seen many times in this book that we can, by careful study, determine the genre, and learn how to understand it in the way in which the original readers would have understood it.

What of the meaning of individual words? These can vary even from one author to another in Scripture. But we have a rich abundance of studies of such words today that there is no problem, provided only that one uses them. But we should not suppose that any modern American, without training, will be competent to study Scriptures because, unfortunately, some of the numerous Scripture study classes today lack competent guides.

For example, an article by this author in *Catholic Biblical Quarterly*, January 1967, pp. 1-19, shows we can recover the meaning of the Hebrew word *hesed*, which was lost when the Scriptures were translated into Greek. Greek had no such word.

Mysterium Ecclesiae, from the Congregation for Doctrine (June 24, 1973), says: "The meaning of the pronouncements of faith depends partly on the expressive power of the language used at a certain point in time and in particular circumstances." (This is, of course, another example of time-conditioned language.)

Of course this is true. It merely means that the resources of the language at a given period may be inadequate for *perfect* expression of divine truth. Hence the document adds: "Moreover, it sometimes happens that some dogmatic truth is first expressed incompletely (but not falsely), and at a later date, when considered in a broader context of faith or human knowledge, it receives a fuller and more perfect expression."[1]

A still further qualification is made by the Sacred Congregation for the Doctrine of the Church: "Finally, even though the truths which the Church intends to teach through her dogmatic formulas are distinct from the changeable conceptions of a given epoch . . . it can sometimes happen that these truths may be enunciated . . . in terms that bear the traces of such conceptions."

An obvious example is the use of the word transubstantiation by the Council of Trent to describe the change of the entire substance of the bread and wine into the substance of the Body and Blood of Jesus. Many of those at the Council doubtless believed the theory of Aristotle about substance and accidents, and that fact influenced the language. However, this does not mean that the Church is committed to the theory of Aristotle. No, the word *substance* can be used in a nontechnical, everyday sense, and the meaning will be the same. Hence the Council of Trent, aware of this fact, used careful language: "This change is fittingly and properly called transubstantiation by the Catholic Church."

So from this instance occurring in the Council of Trent we can gather something very important. Even if we know the thought-world of the Fathers of a Council, the divine protection covers only what they *explicitly* state in writing, not what we just happen to know was *in their minds*. Aristotelianism was in their minds, but they did not *teach* Aristotelianism, even though they borrowed words from it, words which yet could be understood outside of Aristotelianism, as part of the everyday language of that time.

We happen to know that some writers of conciliar texts, during and after the time of St. Augustine, had in mind his unfortunate theory of predestination. Yet Providence prevented them from explicitly teaching it in writing, and it did not become part of our doctrine. We may well surmise, too, that Pope Pius IX may well have had in mind a thought-world that went beyond what he wrote on religious freedom and indifferentism. But only what he explicitly taught counts as the teaching of the Church.

Again, the framers of the Vatican II *Declaration on Religious Liberty* may have held ideas beyond what they explicitly taught. Those ideas are not part of official teaching. Similarly, if an Old Testament writer, or even a New Testament writer, held erroneous ideas but did not explicitly *assert* them in Scripture, they are not part of the teaching of Scripture. Revelation was incomplete before Christ, so some writers may have believed error; but only what they explicitly taught counts.

Because of this historical situation, the documents of *Mysterium Ecclesiae* adds: "The dogmatic formulas of the Church's Magisterium were from the very beginning suitable for communicating revealed truth and . . . they remain forever suitable . . . to those who interpret them correctly. . . . For this reason theologians seek to define exactly the intention of teaching proper to the various formulas."

Words change in meaning over time. Thus the word *sacramentum* meant something different in the first centuries from what it meant in texts of the Council of Trent. So we should study the usage of words at the time an official statement was made. In so doing, we will observe the reservations expressed above. Even if we know that the thought-world of the writers went further than what they explicitly taught in writing, we must not let this knowledge lead us to think they have taught what they did not teach, what they only kept in their minds.

One could even say there is a sort of divine brinkmanship. For God needs to honor two commitments simultaneously. On the one hand, He has given free will; on the other hand, He has promised to protect the teaching of the Church. In doing both at the same time, it is sometimes necessary to draw a very tight line, conceding much to each claim, yet allowing no contradiction.

If, then, we wish to speak of time-conditioning in the words of Scripture without going beyond the lines just drawn, we do positively well. But if we go beyond those boundaries, we soon reach the realm of error.

The 1964 Instruction adds a few valuable admonitions at the end. "Those who instruct the Christian people by sacred preaching," the Instruction says, "need the greatest prudence. . . . They must altogether abstain from futile novelties and things insufficiently proved. As to new opinions that are already solidly proved, they may present them cautiously if necessary, taking into account the characteristics of their hearers. When they narrate biblical events, they must not add fictitious things that are out of conformity with the truth.

"This virtue of prudence must especially be cultivated by those who write for the faithful at the popular level. . . . They must consider it a sacred duty never to depart in the least from the common doctrine and tradition of the Church. Yes, they may turn to their own use the real advances in biblical knowledge . . . but must avoid altogether the rash fancies of innovators. They are strictly charged not to give in to a dangerous itch for novelty, recklessly disseminating attempts at the solution of difficulties without prudent sifting and serious discrimination—disturbing the faith of many."[2]

Vatican II's *Constitution on Divine Revelation* repeats part of the 1964 Instruction but in no way goes beyond it or beyond previous official teachings about Scripture.

Chapter 23

Examples of Form and Redaction Criticism

Examples of form and redaction criticism demonstrate how some of the leading critics actually have worked in this method. They will also show the degree of subjectivity that is characteristic of such critics. Some of them, recognizing the lack of objectivity in their work, have abandoned the entire historical-critical method, of which form and redaction criticism are important parts.

We already saw (chapter 21) how R. Brown and C. F. Evans frankly admit their inability to know why Mark was written or to distinguish between Mark's redactions and the traditions that came down to him. Here are some striking confessions by Rudolf Bultmann, the father of New Testament form criticism. Talking about how to resolve a controverted question of biblical interpretation, he said, "Naturally enough, our judgment will not be made in terms of objective criteria, but will depend on taste and discrimination."[1] In fact: ". . . conclusive knowledge is impossible in any science or philosophy."[2] Even faith should have no real foundation, according to Bultmann, since "security can be found only by abandoning all security."[3] Referring to the search for objective proofs, Bultmann says, "The old quest for visible security . . . is sin."[4] And: "The word of preaching confronts us as the word of God. It is not for us to question its credentials. It is we who are questioned."[5]

In Luke 3:10-14, various kinds of people ask St. John the Baptist what they should do. Bultmann, in spite of his admissions, feels certain here. "This is a catechism-like section," he says, "naively put into the Baptist's mouth, as though soldiers had gone on a pilgrimage to John. There is one thing that makes it improbable that we are here dealing with a product of the primitive Christian Church—that the profession of a soldier is taken for granted. Neither does this passage appear to be Jewish. It is perhaps a relatively late Hellenistic product, developed (by Luke himself) out of the saying from the tradition in v. 11."[6]

Bultmann is sure that the primitive Church could not approve of soldiers. He thinks it must have been totally pacifistic, even though Jesus Himself, when the centurion came to ask Him to cure his servant, praised the centurion: "Not even in Israel have I found such faith" (Matthew 8:10). Nor did Jesus tell him to give up the army. Neither did the angel, in Acts 10:1-9, who was sent to Cornelius the centurion, tell him to give up soldiering.

Bultmann here is using the criterion, discussed in chapter 20, of dual irreducibility (something is from Jesus, or at least level one if it fits neither Jewish ideas nor those of the primitive Church). Yet he does not accept the result of the criterion but calls the verse a "relatively late Hellenistic product developed by Luke himself." Incidentally, especially because of the studies of Martin Hengel, most scholars now think we cannot call something late because it seems Hellenistic, since we now think that "even in Jewish Palestine, in the New Testament period, Hellenistic civilization had a long and eventful history behind it" (*Judaism and Hellenism: Studies in Their Encounter in Palestine During the Early Hellenistic Period*, SCM Press, 1974).

Another prominent critic, Norman Perrin, has different comments on John the Baptist and thinks the saying in Matthew 11:12 about the kingdom of heaven suffering violence from the days of John the Baptist is genuine. The tradition about John the Baptist, he says, shows "a continuous 'playing down' of the role of the Baptist" (*Rediscovering the Teaching of Jesus*, Harper & Row, N.Y., 1967, p. 75).

Perrin thinks the primitive Church was in rivalry with the followers of the Baptist and so would never have made up the saying in Matthew 11:12. In regard to the words that the kingdom of God suffers violence, Perrin adds: "What we have here is the reverse of the situation envisaged in the interpretation of the exorcism: there the kingdom of Satan is being plundered, here, that of God" (p. 77). The real sense seems to be that the Pharisees forcefully try to prevent people from entering the kingdom.

Perrin mentions a saying about exorcisms in Matthew 12:28: "But if it is by the Spirit of God that I cast out demons, then the kingdom of God has come upon you." On page 64, he comments: "The saying has high claims to authenticity. . . ." Perrin then quotes Bultmann,[7] who thinks the saying "is full of that feeling of eschatological power which must have characterized the activity of Jesus."

Perrin makes a shocking blunder on page 16 of the same work. He was once inclined, he says, to believe that the Gospels were historical, but form criticism showed him over and over again they were not: "We would claim that the gospel materials themselves have *forced* us [emphasis added] to change our mind." Perrin says that he has been particularly influenced by Mark 9:1 and its parallels. Mark 9:1 says: "Truly, I say to you, there are some standing here who will not taste death before they see the kingdom of God come with power." Matthew 16:28 is the same, except that it says they will see "the Son of Man coming in his kingdom." Luke 9:27 says that they will see "the kingdom of God."

Perrin believes that Matthew and Mark expect the end soon but that Luke, because he no longer does, rewords things in such a way as to face "the long haul of history." Behind this claim lies the belief that Jesus was in error, expecting the end soon, and that Paul held a similar error.

Perrin thinks he is "forced" to see Matthew and Mark clashing with Luke, but he is not at all forced. The passage could refer to the Transfiguration. More likely, Mark means that they will see the kingdom—the Church—coming, being spread by the power of the Holy Spirit, by miracles after Pentecost. Many scholars today accept at least a partial equation of the Church with the kingdom (see *Jerome Biblical Commentary* II, David M. Stanley and John McKenzie, pp. 783 and 64; *Matthew*, Anchor Bible, 1971, Doubleday, W. F. Albright and C. S. Mann, pp. lxxxvi and c). Note, too, that in the parables of the net (Matthew 13:47-50), of the wise and foolish virgins (Matthew 25:1-13), and of the weeds in the wheat (Matthew 13:24-30), *kingdom* must mean the *Church*. For if it meant *reign*, there would be wicked persons in it; they refuse to subject themselves to God's reign.

When Matthew says that they will see the Son of Man coming in His kingdom, he means that Jesus will *visit* His Church (concept of

Hebrew *paqad*, "to come to help or to punish"—not necessarily visibly). As to Luke, he says that they will see the kingdom, the Church, established.

So Perrin is not at all forced. And again, subjectivity is showing with full power!

This notion that Luke is settling down to the "long haul" basically comes from Hans Conzelmann in his *Die Mitte der Zeit*, 1954 (English title: *The Theology of St. Luke*, Faber & Faber, London, 1961), a work that, though often called "epoch-making," introduced a major error.

We recall (chapter 16) that Fuller now thinks that the historical-critical method is bankrupt. He once felt otherwise. A really great influence has been exercised by his form-critical analysis of Mark 8:29-33, the scene of the confession of Peter at Caesarea Philippi (*The Foundations of New Testament Christology*, R. H. Fuller, Charles Scribner's Sons, N.Y., 1965, p. 109). Jesus asks the disciples who men say that He is. They report various ideas. He then turns to the Apostles and asks them. Peter replies, "You are the Messiah" (unit 1). Jesus then commands them to tell no one (unit 2) and goes on to predict His passion, to which Peter objects (unit 3). Finally He turns on Peter saying, "Get behind me Satan" (unit 4).

Units 1 and 4 seem genuine to Fuller, but he attributes units 2 and 3 to the Church. Unit 2 is the "Messianic Secret." Jesus never said He was Messiah, Fuller writes. "The Church later, being embarrassed, covered by picturing Him as knowing but calling for silence on His Messiahship."

In his analysis, Fuller leans on the work of Wilhelm Wrede (*The Messianic Secret*, tr. J. Greig, James Clark Co., Cambridge & London, 3rd ed., 1971). Wrede tries to prove his point by examples. His strongest case is that in which Jesus raises the daughter of Jairus, then tells the people to tell no one. Wrede explains that since anyone will be able to see that the girl is alive, there is fakery by the Church. But the reply is easy. Jesus was alone in the house with the parents, Peter, James, and John. Had the crowds found out, they would have seized Him, proclaimed Him King Messiah, according to their false notion of what the Messiah should be. Jesus needed silence only long enough to slip out of the house and be on His way.

In unit 3, Jesus predicts His Passion; but, the critics object, when He died and rose, the Apostles acted as if they had never heard of it. So the Church invented the prophecies after the fact. But it is well known that if one has a mental framework and then hears something that does not fit it, that item of information will not enter his mind at all.

Examples are countless. Dr. Semmelweis, in the nineteenth century, found that by taking antiseptic precautions puerperal fever could be largely prevented. His medical colleagues considered it ridiculous, not knowing there were such things as germs. Poor Semmelweis was sent— by doctors—to an insane asylum for the rest of his life. Teilhard de Chardin dreamed of a glorious period, just before Christ's return at the end, when most of the world would be united in love. He must have read Scripture—Luke 18:8, Matthew 24:12, Timothy 3:1-7—but it did not penetrate his thinking (*Consciousness of Christ*).

Having eliminated, as they think they have, units 2 and 3, the critics will then read what they think is the truth without fakery: Jesus asks the Apostles who they say He is. Peter answers that He is the Messiah. Jesus, with the words "Get thee behind me, Satan," angrily rejects the notion that He is the Messiah. This analysis is one of the chief supports of the notion that Jesus was ignorant of His own identity. What a poor proof!

A less radical, but not yet sound, view of the Passion prophecies is found in J. Jeremias's *New Testament Theology* (Charles Scribner's Sons, N.Y., 1971). Jeremias speaks of the three Passion prophecies in the Gospels and says that the third one, Mark 10:33ff. and parallels, so closely matches the actual event, even in details, "that there can be no doubt that this passion prediction is a summary of the passion formulated after the event" (p. 277).

Jeremias admits a core of truth but thinks that the abundance of details is evidence that some falsification has taken place. Behind his theory lurks a disbelief in the possibility of real prophecy. Jeremias also argues that in the first of these prophecies, Mark 3:31, the use of the Greek *dei* is striking. He says that the Semitic languages have nothing that exactly corresponds to it. This, he says, indicates that the first prediction took its form in a Hellenistic milieu. (*Dei* plus accusative and infinitive means "it is necessary that.")

It is now known that Hellenistic influence had been around long before the time of Jesus, so it cannot be argued for that reason that the form is late. It is true that Hebrew and Aramaic lack a word equivalent to the Greek *dei*, but those languages do in other ways express the idea that something *must* happen—in the case of the Passion, by the will of the Father. Examples can be seen in Isaiah 38:10, "I must depart," and in Jeremiah 4:21, "How long must I see?" A complete concordance, under the word *must*, will provide other instances of the concept of necessity in the Old Testament.

Already in 1943, L. J. McGinley studied in detail the alleged parallels between the miracles of Jesus and rabbinic or Greek miracles. The differences are so great that one should not agree with Dennis C. Duling, who repeats the error of Bultmann without correcting it: "The narratives about Jesus, like the biographical framework of the total story of Jesus itself, were judged [by Bultmann] to have little actual historical value, though historical events might lie hidden in them. Miracle stories, for example, were so retold that they often sounded like the miracle stories so common in the Greco-Roman world."[8]

Not if one makes close comparisons, as McGinley did.

Fuller also thought that to believe in the virginal conception is to go counter to the Gospel: "But the virginal conception clashes headlong with this earlier Davidic-sonship Christology, for the latter depends on Jesus' *physical* descent from David through Joseph. . . . Both Evangelists [Matthew and Luke] leave the two concepts side by side, thus indicating their concern, not with historical facts, but with Christological affirmation" (p. 195).

Fuller sees "three possible candidates for the creative milieu: (1) Palestinian Aramaic Christianity; (2) Hellenistic Jewish Christianity; (3) Gentile Christianity, from pagan sources. Everything points to (2) as the correct solution. . . . Thus the virginity of Mary is an idea which could only have arisen in the LXX sphere."

LXX stands for the Septuagint, the old Greek translation of the Hebrew Old Testament. It had *parthenos*, "virgin," in Isaiah 7:14, where the Hebrew had *almah*. But *almah*, "young woman" (commonly unmarried) can mean a virgin. So the thought can be found in the Hebrew too. As to Davidic descent, adoption by Joseph is sufficient for that.

Fuller, perhaps realizing his evidence is insecure, tries to show, in note 43 on the next page, that Hellenistic Judaism already had the idea of a virgin birth in the case of Isaac and others. But he uses statements from a different genre—typology or allegory—and strains them badly to make them seem to give cases of virgin birth.

Study of the parables is quite active today. A turning point came in the two volumes of A. Julicher (*Die Gleichnisreden Jesu*, Tubinger, 1888-1889), who insisted that any *allegorical* explanations of a parable

148

in the Gospels could not have come from Jesus Himself. Julicher argued that Jesus used simple comparisons only, not the detailed applications found in allegories, since His main purpose was to illustrate general truths on morality and religion. Julicher did not prove his point, yet many followed him. A major follower of Julicher was C. H. Dodd: *The Parables of the Kingdom*, Charles Scribner's Sons, N.Y., 1st ed. 1935; revised ed. 1961. Dodd, however, did not agree that the parables of the kingdom deal with general moral or religious truths. Rather, they convey the message of the kingdom of God, which Jesus inaugurated.

On page 105, Dodd begins to deal with parables of crisis: faithful and unfaithful servants (Matthew 24:45-51 and Luke 12:42-46); the waiting servants (Mark 13:33-37 and Luke 12:35-38); the thief at night (Matthew 24:43-44 and Luke 12:39-40); and the ten virgins (Matthew 25:1-12). Dodd thinks that these parables have been reapplied, that they deal with the *Sitz-im-Leben* (life situation) of the Church rather than that of Jesus. The Church, according to Dodd, saw itself in the interval between two crises, the Incarnation and the return at the end; while Jesus had in mind a brief period of intense crisis, the coming of God's kingdom.

What are we to think of this? Dodd, of course, gives no real proof. Yet we can admit that the Church, in retelling parables given by Jesus, might well make different applications of them. We saw in chapter 22 that St. Paul at times uses Old Testament texts in a sense different from that of the original context. So the Church could, not unreasonably, do the same with parables, fitting in everything with the message of Jesus.

J. Jeremias, in *The Parables of Jesus* (translated by S. H. Hooke, Charles Scribner's Sons, N.Y., 1955), gives us a minor but helpful bit of light on the parables in view of rabbinic usage: "Most of the rabbinical parables," says Jeremias, "begin with the words: *marshal l^e*. . . . This usage is an abbreviation of . . . 'I will relate a parable to you. With what shall the matter be compared? It is the case with it as with . . .' " (p. 78). Therefore, in Matthew 13:45, the kingdom of God is not really like a merchant but like the pearl in the story of a merchant who finds a great pearl, as we can see from the full form of the introduction to parables.

We have now seen some examples of form and redaction criticism. What is to be said about them? We do not wish to simply discard these techniques, as do those who once abused them (see chapter 16).

Yet it must be said that, compared to the approach through literary genres, form and redaction criticism are not nearly so fruitful. The genre approach yields more good than harm; form and redaction criticism more often lead to errors. Yet there are many good examples. Let us mention just a few.

Norman Perrin (*Rediscovering the Teaching of Jesus*, pp. 140-141) does discover the correct meaning of *faith* in the Gospels. He says that in ancient Judaism, the basic meaning of *faith* was *trust*. "But to the Jews, trust must of necessity issue in obedience." Therefore faith would include absolute trust and complete obedience. Of course, trust presupposes mental belief in the power or mission of Jesus.

Many are puzzled by Mark 13:30: "This generation will not pass away before all these things take place." Form criticism suggests that perhaps, in the original setting, the passage refers just to the fall of Jerusalem in 70 A.D. That is possible, but it is better to say that the Hebrew *dor* can mean a period (here, the Christian regime) and that there can easily be a multiple-fulfillment pattern here, less well marked than in Matthew 24 but present nonetheless. (On multiple fulfillment, see chapter 5.)

Many form and redaction critics, in their study of Luke's use of his sources, have noted how carefully he follows them—an indication of accuracy and reliability. Recall, too, the special study of Luke's Semitisms, summarized in chapter 12, which also shows the meticulousness of Luke's work in translating his sources.

Chapter 24

Other Forms of Criticism

As we saw in chapter 16, quite a few very prominent scholars are now completely giving up the historical-critical method. Quite improperly; they merely did not learn to live within its limitations. Now they are turning to other methods.

Some attempt a psychoanalytic reading of the New Testament, seeking an analogy between the Gospel narratives, especially the parables and miracle stories, and dreams and visions. Each, they think, is a product of preconscious or unconscious factors. Like an analyst with a patient on the couch, these writers search for little gaps, slips, disagreements that may reveal hidden motivations. Some see the behavior of the prodigal son in the Gospel as a living-out of the Oedipal conflict. There is, they think, a possibility of psychoanalyzing Jesus as He is pictured by the Evangelists.

Others are cultivating a sociological analysis of early Christianity and of the New Testament. No doubt, there are some possibilities in this approach, but it surely cannot replace careful study of the text by means of the historical-critical method.

Within this sociological approach, liberation theology is dominant. Bultmann, the pioneer form critic of the New Testament, thought he saw a gap between Jesus as He really was and the Christ the Church preached. We cannot know much for certain of what He really was, Bultmann thinks, so we take Him and His teaching to mean the same as Heidegger's existentialism: original sin means a loss of authentic being, the resolve to go through with life even though it is dismal in a universe that makes no sense.

In a parallel way the radical liberationists (there are milder forms) use Marx the way Bultmann used Heidegger. This results in a most radical reinterpretation of all Christian teaching. Love becomes a preference for the poor coinciding with an option for class struggle; hope becomes confidence in the future; salvation becomes freedom from economic oppression.

But our chief focus now is on structuralism, also called semiotic analysis. Reactions of Scripture scholars run the full gamut. Some, Joseph Fitzmyer, for example, think it just a fad.[1] Others, for example René Laurentin, call it very promising as a method. Yet Daniel Patte, a leading U.S. practitioner, writes: "A first striking characteristic of a structural exegesis is the absence of the traditional semantic concern: the exegesis no longer aims at what the author meant" (*What is Structural Exegesis?*, Fortress, 1976, p. 14). Instead, the exegete tries to uncover the linguistic, narrative, or mythical structure of the text, on the assumption that the author himself was not aware of using complex structures. Further, according to Patte, "the structuralists acknowledge the plurality of 'structural meanings.'"

There are three types, or levels, of structure, according to the structuralists. All are marked by, affected by, "constraints." Patte explains that "a text may be compared to a hand-woven blanket. . . . The 'design effect' is the result of the intentional combination of colored threads. Yet the 'design effect' is also determined by the limited possibilities [constraints] offered by the loom and the set of colored threads available to the artisan" (p. 21). The first level is made up of the structures of the enunciation, which are limited by the constraints brought about by the author, individual, or group, and his/their situation in life. The second level is made up of the cultural structures, which are shaped by the constraints proper to the specific culture in which the author lives. The deepest level is marked by the structures that characterize man as man. It is this deep level that chiefly concerns structuralists.

They believe, too, that the deepest structures are not necessarily apparent but are apt to be expressed in "codes." To break these codes, as it were, one must pay attention to wholes and show the interrelation of their parts.

Almost all structural study of the Bible goes back to a classic essay by Claude Levi-Straus, "The Structural Study of Myth," which now forms part of his *Structural Anthropology* (Basic Books, N.Y., 1963). Levi-Straus is not a biblical scholar but a philosophical anthropologist. He thinks that "the purpose of myth is to provide a logical model capable of overcoming a contradiction" (p. 229). Myths show, he thinks, very similar patterns of plot and some rather standardized structures. For example, Zuni myths he has studied deal in fundamental oppositions: life-death, nature-culture, heaven-earth, God-man. These oppositions are real and cannot be overcome. Yet a myth can, as it were, transcend them by breaking them up, in the sense of replacing them with secondary oppositions that can in a way be thought of as equivalent to the fundamental opposition.

The life-death opposition, where there is no middle or intermediary, cannot in itself be overcome. But a myth can use agriculture to replace life, and warfare to replace death. There is a mediating term possible here: hunting. Hunting uses death to provide life-giving food. So life and death no longer seem in absolute opposition.

Structuralists note that myth systems feature binary opposition, the kinds of opposites just mentioned. Levi-Straus thinks that binary opposition is basic in human thinking.

Rather naturally then, Algirdas Julien Greimas proposed using a semiotic square for analysis (see his basic works, *Semantique structurale*, Larousse, Paris, 1966, and *Du Sens*, Seuil, Paris, 1970). It is ultimately derived from the logical square of Aristotle.

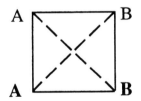

Items A and **B**, connected by diagonals, are contradictories, as are B and **A**. The horizontal lines A to B and **A** to **B** are contraries. The vertical lines, A to **A** and B to **B**, are correlatives. Clearly, thus one can sort out the binary relations with which semiotics is so concerned.

We mentioned above that R. Laurentin thinks this sort of analysis very promising. In his *Les Evangiles de l'Enfance du Christ* (Desclée et Desclée de Brouwer, Paris, 1982, 2nd edition), he devotes 160 pages to a semiotic analysis of the Infancy Gospel of Luke (chapters 1 and 2).

First, he gives a long preliminary (pp. 144-172), in which he classifies at length various statements in the Gospel into categories: grammar, time, several kinds of places, to have, to will, to owe, to know, to see, to be able, to make (with exterior object), to do (without exterior object), to be, etc.

Laurentin next divides the first two chapters of Luke into various narrative programs, that is, sequences of events, and tries to decide what division and grouping is proper (pp. 173-265). Here he admits that structuralists are not in complete agreement. The major groups he settles on are these: annunication to Zachary, Annunciation to Mary, Visitation, birth and circumcision of the Baptist, Birth of Christ the Lord, Presentation in the Temple, Finding in the Temple. Each of these seven is further subdivided.

In his next step Laurentin makes use of the "actantial model" of Greimas. Semiotics bristles with technical terms, most of which could be omitted, as Laurentin shows concretely by his study that makes scant use of them. An "actant" is not the same as an actor. It is a semantic unit (unit of meaning) that comes at a more abstract level than the actor in the usual sense of the word. It can be either singular or plural, abstract or concrete. We can see more easily from the diagram of Greimas, in which there are six actants along three axes:

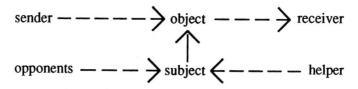

For example, one could identify God as the sender, the Gospel as the object, the receiver as the human race. The opponents are the enemies of Jesus; the helpers are the Apostles, the disciples, and so on. Jesus is the subject who gives the good news.

The use Laurentin makes of this model is as follows: God or Jesus is the sender, he is also the subject. The object is salvation, which is identified with Jesus, who is in that way both subject and object. Laurentin does not identify the opponents. He asserts that Luke does not like to bring out opposition. Helpers, he says, are not yet prominent in this stage of the Gospel. He notes, too, that with one exception, God is the only subject of doing or making with an external object. God brings about activity in humans. He notes, too, that many names of God are given to Christ: Lord, Son of the Most High, Son of God, Savior. The receivers, of course, are the People of God.

Noting that Christ fills all important posts, Laurentin sums up in a manner not found elsewhere. Jesus is at the same time subject and object (Savior and salvation), is identified with God the sender and, in a sense, with men, the receivers. He is God with God, man with men.

In the final stage of his analysis, Laurentin makes use of the semiotic squares.[2] Laurentin works out in great detail the things or statements or persons that fall under the parts of two squares: law and grace, glory and humility. To illustrate, let us follow through the chief points of the law-grace square. Using the same letter designations as in the diagram of the basic square, the law is A, grace is **B**. They are contraries. Then **A** and **B** are, respectively, non-grace and non-law. Thus law and non-law are contradictories; so are grace and non-grace.

Laurentin notes, incidentally, that the word *grace* (not used in Mark, used only three times in John) occurs eight times in Luke and seventeen times in Acts. The word *grace* is also a favorite of St. Paul, with whom Luke associated so much. Laurentin then lists numerous instances of the concept of law in Luke 1 and 2, for example, the observance of justice by Zachary and Elizabeth, the two circumcisions (of John and Jesus), the obedience to the law of Augustus calling for an enrollment. Grace appears, for example, in the benevolence of God to Elizabeth, the coming of the Holy Spirit upon Mary, the Spirit being upon Simeon, and in many more instances.

For the pole of non-grace, Laurentin lists, among other things, the lack of faith in Zachary; the proud, rich, and powerful, who are disgraced in the *Magnificat*; those in darkness mentioned in the *Benedictus*. The pole of non-law includes the enemies of the People of God. In a sense, too, Laurentin sees non-law present, paradoxically, in Mary, who went beyond what the law required. He mentions also that Jesus was "disobedient to His parents by the higher attraction of His Father from heaven." This last item is very regrettable. No less than eleven times in the entire book, Laurentin speaks of Jesus as disobedient—a real irreverence, and a charge that is not at all true. In staying in the temple at age 12, He was not disobeying any command of His parents. He was informally doing what they had not expected. Hence their failure to comprehend; that is, they did not understand this change of pattern from Him, who normally followed their every wish.

It seems that the need to fill out the semiotic square is a chief factor leading Laurentin to this unfortunate repeated statement. Incidentally, one is tempted to wonder if he fully accepts the teaching of the Church that Jesus had the Beatific Vision in His human soul from the moment of conception (see Laurentin, pp. 264, 495).

Laurentin then fills in the three axes (contraries, contradictories, correlatives). He asks whether law and grace are really contraries, and answers that they are in the sense that they differ in having interior and exterior norms, in rule and freedom. But he thinks that the dramatic opposition St. Paul makes of law and grace is resolved and surpassed, for example, in that Jesus was presented in the temple as under the law but is shown by the law itself as the Holy One to come (Luke 2:23).

Laurentin says that the other contraries, non-law and non-grace, are found in the enemies who hate. He adds that this point is not important.

As to the contradictories, grace and non-grace are shown, for example, in the revolution worked by the grace of God in favor of the poor; in the punishment of Zachary, who resisted grace and was punished; and in the prophecy of Simeon, who says that Christ will occasion both the rise and fall of men. Laurentin sees the contradiction of law and non-law in the opposition between the People of God and the pagans to whom the Messiah brings the light. This opposition will be overcome by grace.

As to the correlations: law and non-grace are found in the case of Zachary; grace and non-law appear in the singular paradoxes in which the drive of grace and the movements of the Spirit upset norms and usages. Regrettably, Laurentin mentions again the "disobedience" of Jesus here.

Laurentin also works out the topographical implications of the square so that Nazareth stands for grace, Jerusalem for law, Bethlehem for non-law, and those in darkness (Luke 1:79) for non-grace.

The final part of the working out of the law-grace square is in the modalization of being: seeming-to-be. This is really a subsquare with being and seeming-to-be as A and B, while A and B are, respectively, not seeming-to-be and not being. Across the top line, from A to B, he writes *truth*; across the bottom line, *falsity*. On the vertical lines for correlatives he puts on the left, *secret*, on the right, *lie*. He notes that this square coincides partly with the law-grace square. Laurentin fills in, in some detail, the things that apply to all points here, just as he did with the law-grace square.

Laurentin gives a full treatment also to the second square: glory-humility. A and B are theophany and poverty; **A** and **B** are non-poverty and non-theophany.

In the conclusion, Laurentin, after noting that the constant movement in Luke 1 and 2 is the surpassing of an ordinary and terrestrial program by a divine program, makes three principal points: (1) Zachary and Elizabeth appear at first as models of keeping the law. Yet their modeling is not fully successful: they are freed from sterility, but Zachary becomes mute and Elizabeth remains silent for some time. Next in time comes the gift of the Spirit, who fills the Baptist before his birth, then Elizabeth, then Zachary. The triple gift of the Spirit is especially found in Mary, who stands for grace. (2) The birth of Jesus at Bethlehem, the messianic place, is programmed, not by the law of God, but by the law of Augustus. Glory then follows on grace. The glory that shone on the shepherds stands for God, who is often called glory in the Old Testament; Simeon, in calling Jesus the glory of the people Israel, indicates His divinity. (3) The two scenes in the temple stand also for the passage from law to grace. Jesus at the Presentation is under the law but is manifested by the law itself (Luke 2:23 calls Him "the Holy One"). By the Spirit, Simeon recognizes in Him the salvation, the light of the nations, the glory of Israel. The final scene transcends the others. Jesus, following law and custom, goes to Jerusalem, frees Himself from His parents in disobedience (!), and announces that He belongs to the Father. Then He goes back to daily submission at Nazareth, where He grows under the sign of grace (Luke 2:52 and 2:40). Thus "grace" completes Luke 1-2. It was there at the start; it is there at the end.

Laurentin adds two final observations: (1) The transcendent being of the Son of God is marked from the point of departure in 1:32-35, and appears in progressive manifestations (Annunciation, Visitation, Christmas, theophany in the temple). In the temple, He expresses His Being and mission as Son of God—He passes from merely being to also seeming-to-be—but the full manifestation of that comes later in the Gospel. (2) The theophanies of the infancy are without human glory. They come in the poverty with which the Son of God identified Himself. So we see the unsoundable depth of newness of the Gospel revelation.

This has been a long review of the semiotic analysis done by Laurentin, yet it is merely a summary. But it is a rather good example of how this analysis can be done. Now we must ask ourselves, Of all the items mentioned (and not mentioned) in our summary, which could not have been seen without all the semiotic apparatus? It is doubtful that there is even one, though, admittedly, good insights have been presented.

Not all semiotic analyses turn out even this well. E. R. Leach gives us one in "Genesis as Myth" (in *Myth and Cosmos*, ed. J. Middleton, University of Texas Press, 1967, pp. 1-13).

Leach remarks that in the first creation story of Genesis, though creatures are told to be fruitful and multiply, the narrative nevertheless does not trace the problems of life-death and incest-procreation. These, however, are dealt with in the second creation story, which begins with the opposition heaven-earth. This opposition, writes Leach, "is mediated by a fertilizing mist . . . which blurs the distinction life-death."

The second creation story also reveals oppositions: man-garden, tree of life-tree of death. Eve, in the second story, replaces the creeping things of the first story. "These creeping things," writes Leach, "were anomalous, that is, mediating or holy, in regard to fish, fowl, cattle, and beasts." As to Eve, Leach says that she is "anomalous to the opposition man versus animal." There is still another mediation: the serpent, one of the creeping things, "is anomalous to the opposition man versus woman." Reproduction becomes possible only after the human pair eat the forbidden fruit and, thus, become aware of sexual differences.

In the next stage, the antithesis of the first and last three days of creation in the first narrative reappears in Cain the gardener and Abel the herdsman. Abel's offering of animals is more pleasing to God. Cain's killing of his brother compares with the incest committed by Adam. Hence God's questioning and cursing of Cain, and of Adam and Eve and the serpent, show the same form. "So," says Leach, "Cain's sin was not only fratricide but also incestuous homosexuality."

Still another stage is discovered by Leach. "Though heterosexual incest is evaded," he writes, "the theme of the homosexual incest in the Cain and Abel story recurs in the Noah saga when drunken Noah is seduced by his own son, Ham."

Has this analysis uncovered the real meaning of Genesis? Hardly.

Just a word about analysis of the parables, an area being actively pursued in the U.S. at present. Dan O. Via ("Parable and Example Story," in *Semeia*, vol. 1, 1974, pp. 105-133) has taken the parable of the Good Samaritan (Luke 10:30-35) and put it within the actantial model we saw above. Thus the sender is the Samaritan, the object sent is aid and healing, the receiver is the traveler. Then on the lower line, the helper consists of oil, wine, donkey, innkeeper, robbers (!). The subject is again the Samaritan. The opponents are the priest and Levite. (But they did not oppose, they just neglected.) But Via notes that if we took a broader text, Luke 10:25-37, we would get this model: The sender is Jesus, the object is the meaning of *neighbor*, the receiver might be the scribe. On the lower line, the helper is the story, Jesus is the subject, the opponent is Jewish exclusivism represented by the scribe. There is, of course, truth in all this. But where is the added illumination?

John Dominic Crossan suggests (*In Parables*, Harper & Row, 1973, especially pp. 53-78) that just as there is a twofold function of myth—to mediate the reconciliation of a particular contradiction and to create belief in the permanent possibility of reconciliation—so, too, but in contrast the parable on the surface creates a contradiction within a situation in which one feels secure but, on a deeper level, challenges the fundamental principle of reconciliation. So a parable is a story whose artistic surface structure makes it possible for its deep structure to invade us, in direct contradiction to what one expects. So, the coming of the kingdom implies reversal, because the kingdom overturns our security and leaves us in utter insecurity.

What has the Church said about structuralism? Not a thing up to the present.

Chapter 25

Study of Jewish Language and Literature

Why study Jewish culture, civilization, language, literature? Because all but one of the writers of Scripture were Jews. The exception, St. Luke, shows more Semitic influence, in his Greek, than do the Semites themselves. Further, Jesus and His Apostles were all Semites. Clearly, we can hope to learn much of the physical world and the thought world in which Jesus and the scriptural writers lived from a study of Jewish things.

It is now contrary to fashion to write a life of Christ. Admittedly, we cannot be sure of the chronology of His life, yet such works as the *Synopsis of the Gospels* by Aland not only put texts of the Gospels in parallel columns, they also try to give a reasonable estimate of the chronological sequence. One could fill that data in and construct a life of Jesus. Such lives used to be plentiful. We suspect that a large reason for their present scarcity is the huge skepticism injected by Bultmann and others who say that there is a great gap between the Jesus of history and the Christ of faith. Some of these lives in the past, especially that by Edersheim, added a great deal to our knowledge of Jewish customs and Jewish life in general. Further, St. Paul was trained as a rabbi at the feet of the great Rabban Gamaliel I.

At least some knowledge of the language is very fruitful. Really it is necessary for solid research. For example, when we read St. Paul, we must constantly ask, What is the Semitic word he has in his mind? Thus when Paul says "justice," he has in mind the broader concept of the

Hebrew *sedaqah*, the virtue that impels one to follow all morality. And when Paul says "know," he usually thinks of Hebrew *yada*, which means both "know" and "love." When he writes "many," he normally has in mind Hebrew *rabbim*, "the all who are many."

Much Jewish literature is intertestamental, that is, written between the end of the Old and the start of the New Testament. An especially important portion of Jewish literature—which, in time, spreads beyond the intertestamental period as well—is of the apocalyptic type (see chapter 13). Some scholars consider it, not as a separate genre, but merely as literature that is preoccupied with the end of all history. That description, however, does not fit well with all the actual examples. Some of the more important works of this kind are: the Books of Enoch (the first book is probably second century B.C.; the second, probably late first century A.D.; the third, fifth century A.D.); the Apocalypse of Zephaniah (first century B.C. or A.D.); the fourth book of Ezra (also called Esdras, late first century A.D). There are also Apocalypses of Sedrach, Baruch, Abraham, Adam, Elijah, and Daniel.

St. Paul, in writing to the Colossians, the Ephesians, and perhaps the Corinthians, is struggling against opponents whom he does not name. Would that he had. They may well be apocalyptic-type speculators, though they could equally well be a type of Gnostic. Especially in Colossians, Paul counters the claims that we must attend, not only to Christ, but to some spirit powers, or aeons, whom his opponents consider good but whom, we soon see, Paul considers to be evil spirits (see Colossians 2:15).

The names Paul gives groups of these spirits (following his opponents) include principalities, powers, dominations, and so on—names that were once thought to belong to nine choirs of angels but that we now know were used by Gnostics or apocalyptic speculators for other spirit powers.

Another example of apocalyptic thought is in fourth Ezra 7:32, which says that before the Judgment, "the earth shall give up those who are asleep in it, and the chambers shall give up the souls which have been committed to them."[1] The same thought is found in many of the Fathers of the Church—that the souls of the just, even when fully purified, must wait somewhere until the Judgment before they receive the Beatific Vision (for example, in St. Irenaeus, *Against Heresies* 5.31 and in Tertullian, *De anima* 55). Only martyrs attain the Beatific Vision at once after death.

Again, in Luke 13:23, Jesus is asked point blank, "Lord, will those who are saved be few?" We know from apocalyptic that this question was much discussed, as, for example, in fourth Ezra 7:45-61. Answers tended to be pessimistic: few are saved. Now Jesus would hardly want to give the real answer. To say few would lead many to despair; to say the majority would promote laxity. Jesus, therefore, cleverly parries the question. "Strive to enter by the narrow door," He says. He seems to mean: Do not say that we have Abraham as our Father, as if that would suffice for salvation. See Luke 3:8 and also *Genesis* Rabbah 48.7, which says Abraham sits at the gate of hell and will not let any circumcised Jew enter.

We also have quite a bit of testament literature, not as extensive as the apocalyptic but of similar vintage: the Testaments of the Twelve Patriarchs (second century B.C.); the Testament of Job (first century B.C. or A.D.); Testaments of Abraham, Isaac, Jacob (first to third centuries A.D.); Testament of Moses (first century A.D.); Testament of Solomon (first to third centuries A.D.); Testament of Adam (second to fifth centuries A.D.). Some of these are really also apocalyptic in character. There are some clearly Christian passages in the testaments, and also affinities with the Dead Sea Scrolls, so debate still goes on as to whether the testaments are basically Jewish works with Christian interpolations or Christian works employing Jewish sources.[2]

As we noted in chapter 4, we are very fortunate to have Targums. These are ancient Aramaic translations, plus commentary, on the Old Testament. Some of these were officially recognized by the Jewish authorities: Targum Onkelos on the Pentateuch, and Targum Jonathan on the Prophets. In 1949 a Targum Neofiti was discovered in the Vatican Library. It is part of the Palestinian Targum on the Pentateuch, along with the Jerusalem Targum and the Pseudo-Jonathan.

The dates of the Targums are disputed. A respectable scholarly opinion is that of Samson Levey: "The official Targumim are quite circumspect about adducing Messianic interpretations from the Hebrew text. . . . We may conjecture that the reason might be that the official Targumim stem from Maccabean times [second century B.C.], when hope for a restoration of the Davidic kingship could constitute treason to the Hasmomean dynasty" (*The Messiah: An Aramaic Interpretation*, Hebrew Union College, 1974, p. 142). Levey gives us all the Old Testament texts that the Targums see as Messianic. No matter what the date, the Targums do this without the use of hindsight from fulfillment in

Christ. The writers, of course, rejected Christ. Many writers, as we saw in chapter 20, think the Old Testament prophecies would be good only with hindsight.

Levey is admirably honest in saying that "Christians tended to base their arguments against Judaism on verses of Scripture, and the Targum-interpretation of those verses was often deliberately designed to exclude the Christian argument" (p. 152, n. 10). This is clearly the case with the Targum on Isaiah 53, which makes the meek lamb into an arrogant conqueror. (See *Paul: The Theology of the Apostle in the Light of Jewish Religious History*, H. J. Schoeps, tr. H. Knight, Westminster, 1961, p. 129. Schoeps makes the same admission.) Yet Levey gives many Targums that help one to understand prophecies about Christ.

During about a ten-year period starting in 1947, Bedouins found scrolls and fragments of some six hundred manuscripts in eleven caves on the west side of the Dead Sea, about ten miles south of Jericho, near a cite called Qumran. A sectarian community lived there, seemingly from around 135 B.C. to about 31 B.C., and again from about 1 A.D. to about 68 A.D. Most likely these people were one of three sects of Jews described by Josephus as Essenes (*Antiquities* 13.5.9 n. 171). (The other two sects were the more familiar Pharisees and Sadducees.)

The Essenes seem to have fled there in a revolt against Syrian dominance that began under the Maccabees in 167 B.C. But the Essenes disapproved of the Maccabees taking over the high priesthood, and considered Jerusalem profaned. The settlement was interrupted from 31 to 1 B.C., perhaps owing to an earthquake, plus suspicions by Herod. The settlement was finally destroyed by Roman armies in 68 A.D. in the First Jewish War.

At first, grossly exaggerated and distorted reports made it seem that these discoveries would almost destroy Christianity, showing it to be largely a copy of Essenism. No scholar now believes such things. But we have gained much from these finds. Some Targums have been found there. The most important among them is a Targum on Job from Cave 11, probably written in the second century B.C. Still more important, at least parts of nearly all books of the Old Testament have been found at Qumran. Some of these copies are a thousand years older than the best copies we used to have. But this does not mean they are superior.

From the Dead Sea Scrolls we learned that the text of the Hebrew Old Testament was not yet standardized at that time. It existed in more than one form. Standardization came in the second century. Some texts from Qumran agree with the Septuagint, the old Greek translation of the Old Testament that we used to think was rather loose but now see is apt to be precise, in a different version.

We also learned from the Qumran scrolls that some deuterocanonical books—books not in general accepted by ancient Hebrews—which we had before largely in Greek were found in Aramaic (Tobit, for example) or Hebrew (Sirach, for example) at Qumran. We also have from Qumran manuscripts of some well-known apocryphal books, such as Enoch, Jubilees and some of the testaments of the patriarchs. We used to have them, in some cases, only in Ethiopic translated from a Greek translation. Now we have some in the original Aramaic or Hebrew.

Finally, Qumran has yielded some documents written by the Essenes themselves—their rule of life, their visions of God's plans, and their commentaries on some of the Old Testament prophets. These commentaries are of the type called *pesher*. The Essenes updated, for example, Habakkuk, to apply to their own times.

It is especially interesting to notice that the Essenes strongly emphasized the coming of the Messiah and the need for reform. We know that the Essenes stressed celibacy. This shows that celibacy was perceived as a value. It also removes an objection to Mary's resolve of virginity.

Finally we come to the works of the rabbis, recalling, as we said, that St. Paul was trained as a rabbi. His teacher was the great Rabban Gamaliel I. (*Rabban*, a very special title, was not given to all rabbis.) Gamaliel was so great that a maxim of the rabbis says, "When Rabban Gamaliel the Elder died, the glory of the Law ceased and purity and abstinence died" (Sotah 9.15). He intervened on behalf of the Christians in Acts 5:34ff. Gamaliel followed the school of Hillel (from a few decades earlier), which was in general less severe in its interpretations than the school of Shammai. The written law had 613 precepts, but the oral law had many more. The Pharisees considered both of equal authority, in fact: "It is a worse thing to go against the words of the Scribes than the words of the [written] law" (*Sanhedrin* 11.3). We can see the problem when Jesus clashed with these interpretations, though not with the law itself.

The content of the Law was in two categories: *halakah*, norms for living; and *haggadah*, which was mainly historical and largely narrative. The rabbis would deduce many rules for living from the Law, using seven rules of interpretation (hermeneutic) attributed to Hillel, later expanded to thirteen by Rabbi Ishmael. These rules were for the halakah; there were other rules for the haggadah.

At first, all this was transmitted by memory (an echo comes in Sirach 39:1-3). This oral transmission lasted until more than a century after the time of Paul; but near the end of the second century A.D., there was a written collection that won official approval. This collection, called the *Mishnah* ("repetition"), was made by Rabbi Judah na-Nasi (also called Judah the Holy). It contained the decisions up to that time by rabbis who were called the *Tannaim*. Later, further commentary was added from the rabbis called the *Amoraim*, whose writings cover the period from 200 A.D. to about 500 A.D. This commentary was called the *Gemara*. The *Talmud* is formed from the Mishnah (not including tractates, however), and the Gemara (not provided for all tractates). There are two Talmuds, the Babylonian and the Palestinian.

The Mishnah gives decisions that are, for the most part, not explicitly related to Scripture. Hence, in the period of the Tannaim, other interpretations based more directly on Scripture, were made. These are called Halakic Midrashim. Halakah pertains to legal matters. Midrash basically is an investigation of a text to discover its hidden meanings and apply them to new situations. Not all define midrash in the same way. (Compare Hebrew *darash*, "to seek or to examine.") Especially important are the commentary on the legal section of the Exodus (the *Mekilta*); the *Sifra*, on Leviticus; and the *Sifre*, on Numbers and Deuteronomy. The older midrashim—both halakic and nonhalakic—were handed down and developed more, and come down to us in such collections as the *Midrash Rabbah* and other midrashim of homiletic nature.

The Mishnah is divided into six main orders, each of which is subdivided into treatises, making a total of sixty-three treatises.

A doctor of the law would solve cases, in a casuistic way, using decisions thus collected from the most authoritative rabbis, and he would add his own.

Some matter is not just casuistic but almost scrupulous. A whole treatise in the Mishnah is called *Bezah* (egg). Here was one problem: Suppose a hen lays an egg on a festival day following the Sabbath. May one eat the egg? The school of Shammai said one might eat it; the school of Hillel said no. One should not profit by illegal work done by the hen (1:1). Again, suppose a cripple has a wooden leg. Rabbi Meir said he may go out with it on the Sabbath; Rabbi Jose said no (*Shabbath* 6.1.8). Paul would have learned such legal decisions in great numbers.

However, there is another side to Jewish piety, which is warm, shows an appreciation of the Fatherhood and the love of God. (On this aspect, see *Palestinian Judaism in the Time of Christ*, J. Bonsirven, tr. W. Wolf, McGraw-Hill, N.Y., 1965; and *Aspects of Rabbinic Theology: Major Concepts of the Talmud*, Solomon Schechter, Schocken, N.Y., 1969.)

Besides the Mishnah, there is another, still larger, collection, called the *Tosefta*. It consists of additions to the Mishnah. In its present form, it was probably not edited until the fourth century. But the matter on the whole is much older and really forms a sort of supplement to the Mishnah.

In order to use these rabbinic materials as a help in understanding the New Testament, we must first ask about the dates of the material. Some of the material is easily dated, for instance, when the name of the rabbi who made the decision is given. Sometimes we have this form: "Rabbi X said in the name of Rabbi Y." But there are many other sayings, both halakah and haggadah, without any rabbi's name attached. It is likely that most of the anonymous material of the halakic type comes from the period 133-200 A.D. (between Rabbi Akiba and Rabbi Judah ha-Nasi). This, of course, helps. But there is a further problem.

Most of the tradition was formulated and written down after 70 A.D., the date of the fall of Jerusalem. It seems that the legal matter has been mediated through one man, Johanan ben Zakkai, who belonged to the school of Hillel. So much of the legal tradition of the opposite school, that of Shammai, has been lost. The same is probably true of the nonlegal tradition. Until shortly before the Jewish War of 66-70, the school of Shammai was the more influential, yet its thoughts are lost to us. Further, some of what we do have is likely to be from non-Pharasiaic sources.

Even so, given the tenacity of the Jews about their traditions, many scholars think we can assume that ideas found, let us say, a century after St. Paul were current also in his day.

There are cases, of course, in which we can trace an idea both before and after 70 A.D. A specially important example is the concept of sin as a debt. Rabbi Simeon ben Eleazar (late second century) wrote in *Tosefta, Kiddushin* 1.14 (cited from Bonsirven, p. 111): "Happy is the man who has practiced a commandment, for he has tipped the balance toward the side of merit, both for himself and the whole world. But woe to the man who has committed a transgression, for he has tipped the balance to the side of debt (*hobah*), both for himself and the world." Notice both the debt concept and solidarity.

Much the same thought is found in Rabbi Akiba (50-135 A.D.), in *Pirke Aboth* 3:20. Akiba speaks of the divine shopman giving credit and then sending around the collectors to exact payment. The concept of sin as debt was also common in the time of Christ. S. Lyonnet speaks of "the notion widespread in the Aramaic milieu of primitive Christianity: sin considered as a debt" (*Sin, Redemption, and Sacrifice*, Biblical Institute Press, 1970, p. 32). For example, the Targums may use Aramaic *hobah*, "debt," for *sin*. The Greek word *aphienai* is common in the Synoptic Gospels to mean "forgive," but the connotation is that of canceling a debt. In the Our Father (Matthew 6:12), we find Greek *opheilemata*, "debts," for *sins*.

St. Paul, in Colossians 2:14, speaks of Christ as having, by His death, "canceled the bond which stood against us with its legal demands." Farther back, it is at least highly probable that the Hebrew concept of *bisheggagah*, involuntary sin—that is, transgression of a law of God done unwittingly—reflects God's holiness and concern for the moral order that debts be paid even when personal guilt is absent (compare Leviticus 4:27; Genesis 12:17; Luke 12:47-48; 1 Corinthians 4:4).

The purpose here has been to provide a concrete example of how this work can be done to ensure, in a particular case, that a later rabbinic text reflects the thought world of the New Testament. In particular, we think of St. Paul in Colossians 1:24: "Now I rejoice in my sufferings for your sake, and in my flesh I complete what is lacking in Christ's afflictions for the sake of his body, that is the church. . . ."

Now of course, Christ, the individual, lacked no suffering. But the whole Christ, of which Christians are the members, may be lacking (see 1 Corinthians 12:12-13; Colossians 1:18). One member may fail to do his part in rebalancing the scales of which Rabbi Simeon ben Eleazar spoke. But another member can make up for this failure—and Paul feels it part of his duty to do so. This same concept of the objective order is strongly present in the doctrinal introduction to Pope Paul VI's *Indulgentiarum Doctrina*.

The tendency is widespread today to water down the sense of Colossians 1:24, to say that as a matter of fact Paul had to suffer much in preaching the Gospel. Of course he did. But the richer meaning comes out when we set his words against the background of the thought world of Judaism in his time.

168

Chapter 26

Biblical Archaeology

Biblical archaeology is another immense area of study, so large that we can do no more than give an introduction to it. The remains that have been dug up are of two basic kinds, written and unwritten

Genesis 23:3-20 tells us that when his wife, Sarah, died at Hebron, Abraham bought land from the Hittites to use as a burial place. There was once a great Hittite empire in the eastern part of Asia Minor, extending down into Canaan at the point of its greatest expansion (two periods: 1900-1650 B.C. and 1430-1200 B.C.). Some Hittite monuments had already been discovered in the seventeenth century, but it was only in the late nineteenth century that much excavating was done. A German expedition that began in 1906 found Hittite state archives, more than twenty thousand clay tablets written in cuneiform (wedge-shaped writing). The writing was not deciphered until 1915, when the Czech F. Hrozny managed to read the tablets and found that the language was related to Indo-European (the ancestor of most families of languages of Europe and some in India).

Special interest has centered on the Hittite vassal treaties. Pioneer work in this field was done by G. E. Mendenhall (see *Biblical Archaeologist Reader*, vol. 3, pp. 25-53, and D. J. McCarthy, *Treaty and Covenant*, rev. ed., Biblical Institute, Rome, 1978). There are some resemblances in format and wording between such Hittite treaties and the covenant described in Exodus 20 and Joshua 24. However, it does not seem likely that the Hebrews deliberately modeled the covenant on the

Hittite treaties. Similarities are not nearly close enough to require that, and we know similar situations can call forth similar responses.

Ugarit, though not mentioned in the Bible, has yielded a rich find of tablets. It is a city on the Phoenician coast that flourished in the period about 2000-1200 B.C. The modern site is called Ras Shamra. About fourteen hundred tablets in Ugaritic have been found, in a cuneiform that is close to alphabetic.

From the Ugaritic myths we learn how to understand better the language found in Amos 1:3 to 2:8 and Proverbs 30:18-31. Ugaritic often uses a synonymous parallelism wherein a thought is repeated in different words in the next line. The synonym for any number is the number plus 1. Amos 1:3, for example, says, "For three transgressions of Damascus and for four, I will not revoke the punishment." The two numbers are considered the same. Similarly, ten thousand becomes a synonym for one thousand (see *Stories from Ancient Canaan*, ed. and tr. by M. D. Coogan, Westminster, 1978; esp. pp. 14-18).

Since Ugaritic is a Semitic language rather similar in some ways to Hebrew, Mitchell Dahood, in his three-volume commentary on, and translation of, the Psalms (Anchor Bible, 16-17A), thinks he can throw light on, and revise lines of, the Psalms. For there are many words in Hebrew whose meaning is not fully certain (about seventeen hundred words occur only once in the Hebrew Bible). Ugaritic, Dahood thought, could shed light. In Anchor Bible 17A (pp. xli-lii), Dahood's revisions could lead scholars to revise their notions of how early the Hebrews came to know of retribution in the future life. His conclusions have been challenged, but they are still highly probable.

A related development comes from the finds at Ebla (now Tell Mardikh), a city estimated to have had about a quarter of a million people. Uncovered in 1974-1976, it yielded over sixteen thousand tablets, eighty percent of which are in Sumerian, about twenty percent in Eblaite, a Semitic language that, according to Dahood, is closer to Hebrew than is Ugaritic. Unfortunately, the value of the find is still clouded by bitter fighting between Paolo Matthiae, chief archaeologist, and Giovanni Pettinato, first epigrapher of the expedition. Before his early death, in 1982, Dahood worked closely with Pettinato. His proposals can be seen in "Afterword: Ebla, Ugarit, and the Bible" (*The Archives of Ebla*, Doubleday, 1981, pp. 271-321). Many personal names not before known outside the Bible are found in the tablets: Adam, Eve, Jabal, Noah, Hagar, Bilhah, Michael, Israel, and others. Pettinato and Dahood be-

170

lieved that there are theophoric names (names with a divine element built in, such as Mi-ka-ya, "Who is like Ya?") that show Yahweh was known in Ebla long before the time of the Bible. The tablets probably are to be dated 2400-2250 B.C.

The ancient site of Mari, on the Euphrates River, was excavated in the 1930s and 1950s. Mari was great in the period 1750-1697 B.C. King Zimri-Lim, the last king of Mesopotamia there, was a contemporary of the great Hammurabi of Babylon, who was a contemporary of Shamsi-Adad I of Assyria. Since the latter's dates are known, we can date Zimri-Lim. This may well have been the period of Abraham. Twenty thousand clay tablets have been found there.

To the east, and somewhat north of Mari, is ancient Nuzi, excavated in the 1920s. There five thousand cuneiform tablets have been found—several hundred years after the Mari tablets. But the Nuzi tablets shed light on some practices of the patriarchs, for example, Abraham's adoption of the slave Eliezar (Genesis 15:2-3), who was later replaced by Isaac. This is in accord with Nuzi custom. Again, if a Nuzi wife were sterile, she was expected to give her husband a slave concubine to provide children, as we see in Genesis 16:2. These things do not prove that Abraham belonged in this period, but they do help show his historical character.

Fascinating texts also come from Amarna, called Akhtaton in ancient times. Situated on the Nile between Thebes and Memphis, it was the capital of Pharaoh Amenhotep IV, who changed his name to Akhenaton and worshiped the sun disc Aton instead of Amon. Among the 375 items found there are many letters from vassal rulers in Palestine and Syria, some of them almost frantically asking help against the Hapiru, a name similar to *Hebrew*.

The Dead Sea Scrolls, which were reviewed in chapter 25, should also be mentioned. There are other written finds, but now let us turn to the unwritten matter.

Does archaeology prove the Bible is right? While it supports some things, archaeology raises problems about other things. Very many problems cluster around the date of the Exodus, the departure of the Hebrews from Egypt, and deal with the cities they were supposed to have conquered or been involved with soon before or after the entrance of the Hebrews into Canaan.

While in the desert, the Hebrews spent much time around Kadesh-Barnea. But there seems to have been no settlement there until much later, about the tenth century. Then the king of Arad defeated the Hebrews near Hormah. But Arad seems to have been uninhabited c 2700 - c 1100 B.C., and Hormah was not occupied between 1500 and 1200. The Hebrews would have seen these sites in a first attempt to come into the promised land through the Negeb, the south. Later they came around the east side of the Dead Sea and skirted Edom and Moab. The Hebrews conquered the kings of Hesbon and Bashan, and, of course, caused the walls of Jericho to fall. But there are problems: Hesbon was not inhabited in the millennium before 1200, and there was no notable city of Jericho after about 1500. Some archaeological data, however, do agree with the Old Testament. Lachish and Hazor, for instance, were destroyed c 1250-1200.

In chapter 15 it was suggested that probably the genre of the Book of Joshua, which describes much of the conquest, was at least similar to that of epic, an idealized story of the great beginnings of a people. Similarly, it is likely that at least parts of Exodus are somewhat epic in character. Some scholars become so free in their interpretations as to say that Abraham, Isaac, and Jacob were not really grandfather, father, and son, but tribal heads who later were associated in an epic pattern. Further, there are speculations that the Hebrews did not go down into Egypt all at once or leave all at once. Some say that the four major biblical traditions (Exodus-Sinai-Wilderness-Conquest) belonged originally to distinct groups. G. E. Mendenhall thinks that the conquest was just some guerilla campaigns by people already on the scene at the time of a great breakdown of the city cultures in Palestine in the period 1300-1200 B.C.[1]

These proposals are much too radical. Yet genre gives us much freedom here. Exodus 12:38 does tell us that "a mixed multitude also went up with them," that is, with the Hebrews. Further, Joshua 8:30-35 tells how Joshua, after the conquest of Ai, held a great covenant ceremony on Mount Ebal. He seems to have met no interference, though Mount Ebal was near the city of Shechem, the excavations of which show it to have been powerful at that time, though Joshua was not said to have conquered it. Could it be that the Hebrews had friends or relatives already in that area, perhaps Hebrews who were in an earlier segment of the Exodus, or even Hebrews who had not been in Egypt at all? (See *Biblical Archaeology*, G. Ernest Wright, revised 1962, Westminster, pp. 76-77.) An epic genre would be quite capable of taking in these proposals.

The problems cluster around the highly uncertain date of the Exodus. The root of the trouble is that the Old Testament does not give us the name of the Pharaoh who was on the throne when the Exodus took place. This is in accord with normal Egyptian practice. The real name of the king was too sacred; he was a god. *Pharaoh* was used for all kings. Meaning "Great House," the use of the word *Pharaoh* was loosely comparable to our use of "the White House." Other means must be used to date the Exodus.

There have been two groups of theories. One, which has long enjoyed favor, starts with Exodus 1:11, which tells how the Pharaoh oppressed the Hebrews with forced labor: " . . . and they built for Pharaoh store-cities, Pithom and Raamses." Now Ramses II (c 1290-1224 B.C.) moved his capital to the region of the delta and began building projects there, including the city of Raamses. So the Pharaoh of the oppression and of the Exodus would probably be Ramses, which would date the Exodus about 1300-1280 B.C. The next Pharaoh, Merneptah, put up a stele, a monument claiming he had defeated the Hebrews in the Canaan area, around 1220 B.C. Further, it is claimed, the rapid rise of Joseph to become vizier in Egypt is more easily explained if the kings then were the foreign Hyksos (perhaps including Semites), who dominated Egypt c 1730-1570. Then when the Hyksos were expelled and a new dynasty came, there would be a new Pharaoh who "did not know Joseph" (Exodus 1:8). This theory is quite tempting, though the evidence for it is hardly conclusive.

An older theory is again gaining favor. This view starts from 1 Kings 6:1, which says: "In the four hundred and eightieth year after the people of Israel came out of the land of Egypt, in the fourth year of Solomon's reign . . . he began to build the house of the Lord." Now Solomon probably began to reign about 961 B.C., so his fourth year would have been about 957 B.C. On that calculation, the Exodus would have come around 1437 B.C. We must say "around," since the number 480 is the product of 12 x 40—both highly favored numbers in Hebrew approximations.

We should still suppose, nonetheless, that a date sometime in that century is correct, according to this theory. If we accept 1437 B.C. as the approximate date of the Exodus and then add the 430 years that Exodus 12:40 says the Hebrews spent in Egypt, we get around 1867 B.C. for the entrance into Egypt. Some will object that this is too early for the Hyksos. But Joseph gained power with the help of Providence, so there is no need to suppose that favor from foreign-born Hyksos was necessary. Of course, the 430 years in Egypt is only approximate, but the Septuagint translation of the Hebrew says that "the dwelling of the sons of Israel, which they spent in Egypt and in Canaan, [was] 430 years." Galatians 3:17 gives 430 years for the period between the promise to Abraham and the giving of the law on Sinai. Clearly, we cannot press the numbers tightly, knowing the inclination of the Hebrews to use very round numbers. In this connection, the Hebrew of Jonah 3:4 has Jonah threatening destruction to Nineveh in forty days; the Septuagint of the same has three days. It seems the number was round, very round, and the Septuagint translators felt three expressed it better for Greek speakers. (Review the matter of variant traditions, which was explored in chapter 15.) This figure of about 430 years allows us to estimate the approximate period of the patriarchs Abraham, Isaac, and Jacob. These dates fit well with other known data.

This older theory has recently been revived and much improved in a new book by John J. Bimson, *Redating the Exodus and Conquest* (*Journal for the Study of the Old Testament Supplement Series*, vol. 5, University of Sheffield, England, 1978). Bimson places the Exodus at about 1470 B.C. Allowing a full forty years for the wandering in the desert, the fall of Jericho would have been around 1430 B.C. This date, as Bimson shows with new evidence, would fit with all the existing archaeological information on Jericho and many other sites. In fact, a review in *Catholic Biblical Quarterly* (vol. 42, January 1980, pp. 88-90) says: "The MB II C destruction of Jericho is everything one could ask for Joshua. . . . And so it goes down the list of relevant sites, with the exception of Ai and Heshbon." Bimson replies, (p.64), that we need not identify the later village of Ai with the one destroyed by Joshua, and, (p. 69), that Heshbon need not have been a fortified site at the time of Joshua.

Kenneth Kitchen, of the University of Liverpool, adds some helpful observations in *The Bible in Its World: The Bible and Archaeology Today* (InterVarsity Press, Downers Grove, Illinois, 1977, pp. 10-15). Kitchen notes that the mud-brick buildings of the ancient Near East could gradually have been swept away by wind, sand, and rain. Further, excavations are very costly, and not always is a site completely excavated. For example, ancient Ashdod covers about seventy acres of lower city area and another twenty acres of acropolis. But by 1977 only one and a half acres had been excavated. As to the site of Ai, only a tenth of the site of Et-Tell (supposed to be Ai) had been excavated. Only a small portion of Jericho has been excavated. There can also be site shift. When people no longer could live comfortably on the crest of their mound, they might move to an adjoining area or some small distance away. This could happen more than once. Jericho was abandoned from Hellenistic times, and moved to near the springs of Ain-Sultan, onto the site that became modern Jericho (Er-Riha). But in Hellenistic and Roman times, palaces and villas were constructed at still a third site nearby (Tulul Abu el-Alaiq). So today there are three "Jerichos."

R. Brown admits this site shift in regard to Arad (whose king defeated the Hebrews near Hormah). He writes in *Recent Discoveries and the Biblical World* (Glazier, Wilmington, 1983, pp. 68-69): "Aharoni, the excavator," he writes, "argues that in Canaanite times Arad was not at Tell Arad but at Tell el-Milh (Malhata), 7 miles southeast of Tell Arad, while Hormah was at Khirbet el-Meshash (Masos), 3 miles further west."

So we see that archaeology at times supports the Old Testament; at times raises problems. But the problems can be solved—some by an application of the principles of genre, some by adopting the chronology proposed by Bimson, some by the use of Kitchen's principles. So there is really no need to have recourse to the extreme reconstructions of Exodus-Sinai-Wilderness-Conquest that some propose, even though by supposing an epic genre most, if not all, of these proposals could be digested.

175

EPILOGUE

Early in our study we saw that only six easily observable facts are needed to prove that the teaching authority of the Church comes from Jesus. That Church, in turn, assures us that there is no error at all in Scripture.

With the help of the new techniques, we can see that the Church is completely right. Numerous problems that early in this century would have seemed unsolvable have been solved.

In regard to the methods themselves, some think that only highly trained specialists can understand them. These people are too easily awed. Anyone can grasp at least the basics of these methods, and more too. These methods are not mysterious or formidable. They are our friends. They help us understand Scripture more fully. They make it possible for us to defend its complete inerrancy.

NOTES

Chapter 2

1. Translated by E. W. Leverenz and R. Norden, published by the major Lutheran House Concordia in 1937.
2. Eusebius, *Church History*, 4.3, 1.2.

Chapter 3

1. See Pope John Paul II, *Original Unity of Man and Woman, Catechesis on the Book of Genesis* (Boston: St. Paul Editions, 1981), the audiences of September 12, 1979, September 19, 1979, January 2, 1980.

Chapter 6

1. "Inspiration, Normativeness, Canonicity and the Unique Sacred Character of the Bible," *Catholic Biblical Quarterly* (July 1981), pp. 447-469.
2. "Bultmann replies to his critics," *Kerygma and Myth*, Vol. I, 2nd ed., ed. Hans W. Bartsch, trans. Reginald H. Fuller (London: SPCK, 1964), p. 210.
3. Ibid., pp. 1-44, especially pp. 26-28.
4. Ibid., p. 19.
5. "Sacred Character of the Bible," p. 457.
6. *Jerome Biblical Commentary*, Vol. II, 2nd ed., ed. R. E. Brown et al. (New York: Prentice Hall, 1968), p. 218.

Chapter 7

1. *Enchiridion Biblicum* (Arnodo, Romae, 1954), p. 81ff.
2. Vatican II, *Constitution on Divine Revelation*, n. 11.
3. See A. Grillmeier, "The Divine Inspiration and Interpretation of Sacred Scripture" in *Commentary on the Documents of Vatican II*, Vol. III, ed. H. Vorgrimler (New York: Herder & Herder, 1969), p. 213.
4. The early Fathers of the Church refer to it many times, for example, *Shepherd of Hermas*, Parable 9.16.5; St. Justin, *Dialogue with Trypho* 72; St. Irenaeus, *Against Heresies* 3.20.4; Clement of Alexandria, *Stromata* 6.6; St. Athanasius, *Ad Epictus* 6; Origen, *On Romans* 5.1, and many, many more. St. Thomas Aquinas teaches that in his *Summa, Suppl.* 69.7c.

Chapter 8

1. Wilfred Harrington, *Mark* (Wilmington: Glazier, 1979), p. 47.
2. Vatican II, *Constitution on Divine Revelation*, n. 11.

3. See chapters 20-23.
4. Revised Standard Version has the number Joel 3:10.

Chapter 9

1. We studied the passage in chapter 7 and saw that it rules out error. For the Cardinal's words and later events, see A. Grillmeier, "Dogmatic Constitution on Divine Revelation, Chapter III," *Commentary on the Documents of Vatican II*, Vol. III, ed. H. Vorgrimler (New York: Herder & Herder, 1969), pp. 204-215.
2. Vorgrimler, *Documents of Vatican II*, pp. 205-206.

Chapter 10

1. *Enchiridion Biblicum*, pp. 456-458.
2. *People's Almanac* (Garden City, New York: Doubleday, 1975), p. 1339.
3. A. Parrot, *Nineveh and the Old Testament*, 2nd ed. (New York: Philosophical Library, 1955), pp. 85-86.
4. H. Deizinger and A. Schonmetzer, *Enchiridion Symolorum Definitionum et Declarationum* (Herder, Friburg: Brisyoviae, 1963, 32nd ed.), n. 2866.
5. See W. Most, *New Answers to Old Questions* (London: St. Paul Publications, 1971), pp. 88-112, especially pp. 106-108.

Chapter 11

1. Deizinger and Schonmetzer, *Enchiridion Symbolorum*, n. 3896.
2. Pope John Paul II, *Original Unity of Man*.
3. Ibid., p. 63.
4. Ibid., p. 64-65.
5. Ibid., p. 68.
6. Deizinger and Schonmetzer, *Enchiridion Symbolorum*, n. 1514.

Chapter 12

1. A. Wright, *The Literary Genre Midrash* (Staten Island: Alba House, 1967).
2. *National Catholic Reporter* (December 2, 1977), p. 10.
3. W. Most, *Journal for the Study of the New Testament*, Vol. 15 (July 1982), pp. 30-41.
4. The full force of these words appears from the history of the debates at the Council on the passage cited. See Beda Rigaux, "Dogmatic Constitution on Divine Revelation: The New Testament," Vorgrimler, pp. 252-261, especially 256-261.

5. See Robert R. Wilson, "Between 'Azel' and 'Azel': Interpreting the Biblical Genealogies," *Biblical Archaeologist* 42.1 (Winter 1979), pp. 11-22.

Chapter 14

1. The texts of Amenemopet cited can be found in J. B. Pritchard, *Ancient New Eastern Texts (Princeton, New Jersey: University Press*, 1955), pp. 421-424, or in Jack Finegan, *Light From the Ancient Past*, 2nd ed. (New York: Princeton, 1974), pp. 124-125. Finegan gives texts of Proverbs and Amenemopet in parallel columns.

Chapter 18

1. Sammaciccia-Burakowski, *The Eucharistic Miracle of Lanciano* (Fort Worth, Texas: Stella Maris, 1976).
2. For details, see W. Most, *The Consciousness of Christ* (Front Royal, Virginia: Christendom College Press, 1980), pp. 15-17.

Chapter 19

1. K. A. Kitchen, *Ancient Orient and Old Testament* (Downer's Grove, Illinois: InterVarsity Press, 1966), pp. 112-134. On the claims that the traditions are not reliable, or early, see K. A. Kitchen, *The Bible In Its World* (Downer's Grove, Illinois: InterVarsity, 1977).
2. A table of these is found in Bernard Orchard, *Matthew, Luke and Mark* (Manchester: Koinonia Press, 1976), pp. 86-87. A detailed analysis of the case is found in the work cited by Farmer, chapter 4. Lists can be found in the work by Stoldt, pp. 276-280 and 274-275.
3. "The Semitisms of St. Luke's Gospel," *Journal of Theological Studies*, Vol. 44 (1943), p. 130.
4. *Graecitas Biblica*, ed. 4 (Romae: Pontificium Institutum Biblicum, 1960), par. 361.
5. "Bultmann's Law of Increasing Distinctness," *Current Issues in Biblical and Patristic Interpretation*, ed. G. F. Hawthorne (Grand Rapids, Michigan, 1975), pp. 196-210. See also *The Tendencies of the Synoptic Tradition*, ed. E. P. Sanders (New York: Cambridge University Press, 1969).

Chapter 20

1. Raymond Brown, "The Myth of the Gospels without Myth," *St. An-*

thony's Messenger, May 1971, pp. 45-46. On miracles, see articles by L. Sabourin in *Biblical Theology Bulletin*, 1971, pp. 59-80; 1974, pp. 115-175; 1975, pp. 146-200; 1972, pp. 281-307.

2. Raymond Brown, *The Virginal Conception and Bodily Resurrection of Jesus* (New York: Paulist, 1973), p. 31, n. 37.

3. Ibid., p. 66.

4. James Mackey, *Jesus the Man and the Myth* (New York: Paulist, 1979), p. 286. On the resurrection, see L. Sabourin, *Biblical Theology Bulletin*, 1975, pp. 262-293.

5. Brown, "The Myth of the Gospels."

6. Joseph A. Fitzmyer, *A Christological Catechism: New Testament Answers* (New York: Paulist, 1981), p. 36.

7. Jacob Neusner, *Messiah in Context* (Philadelphia: Fortress, 1984). See also William Most, "The Knowledge of Our Lady," *Faith and Reason* XI (1985), pp. 51-76.

Chapter 21

1. We called these mini-genres—in contrast to the larger kinds of genres which we surveyed in the early chapters of this book. These larger kinds had more extensive consequences as to how we should understand things; these mini-genres have lesser consequences. Yet in both cases, we should study them.

Chapter 22

1. The reason is that divine truths are often simply beyond the power of human language to express fully. So the Church may make a pronouncement that is not false but yet is not perfect, does not exhaust the possibilities of the divine revelation. That will leave room for an improved expression later on. However, this will not mean there is anything positively wrong with the early statement.

2. What would the Instruction think of one who not only proposes rash things but ridicules all attempts to defend the truth of a certain passage of Sacred Scripture as "an unmitigated disaster"? (See chapter 7.)

Chapter 23

1. Rudolph Bultmann, *The History of the Synoptic Tradition*, tr. John Marsh (New York: Harper & Row, 1963), p. 47.
2. *Kerygma and Myth*, Vol. I, ed. Hans Bartsch, 2nd ed. (London, SPCK, 1964), p. 195.
3. Ibid., p. 210.
4. Ibid., p. 19.
5. Ibid., p. 41.
6. Bultmann, *Synoptic Tradition*, p. 145.
7. Ibid., p. 162.
8. "Hellenic Analogies and the Typical Healing Narrative," *Theological Studies*, Vol. 4 (1943), pp. 385-419, summarized in *The Consciousness of Christ*, pp. 218-219.

Chapter 24

1. Joseph Fitzmyer, *Christological Catechism* (New York: Paulist Press, 1982), p. 121.
2. He first outlines what others have proposed: The Group of Lyon (CADIR), the Association de la Roche-Colombe (Paris), and Agnes Gueret. He is closest in his views to the latter.

Chapter 25

1. Cited from *The Old Testament Pseudepigrapha*, ed. James H. Charlesworth (Garden City, New York: Doubleday, 1983), p. 538.
2. For all of these, and for many more nonscriptural Jewish works, we are fortunate to have the solidly scholarly two-volume work edited by Charlesworth, cited above.

Chapter 26

1. G. E. Mendenhall, *The Tenth Generation: The Origins of the Biblical Tradition* (Baltimore: John Hopkins, 1973).

GLOSSARY

Apocalyptic A pattern of writing (genre, see pp. 49-51) which uses heavy imagery and describes secret revelations (explained on pp. 75-76).

Aristotelianism The philosophy of Aristotle, a Greek (384-322 B.C.). His work was scarcely known to the Fathers of the Church, but was used extensively by St. Thomas Aquinas.

Bible criticism Same as historical-critical method. It has been in vogue for about two centuries now. It examines everything in a text with great care, seeking to put it into its original, historical setting. It seldom proves anything conclusively, since it relies mostly on internal evidence (from within the text itself). Some who were once overconfident in it (not seeing its limits) are now overreacting by discarding it completely (see chapter 16).

Demythologize To remove the "mythical" element from a text, especially from the Gospels (see myth below). The pioneer of this approach was Rudolf Bultmann (*Form Criticism of the Gospel*, 1919). This approach was marked by much subjectivity and rejection of the supernatural, and belief in the "creativity" of the community. (Detailed description and criticism in *The Consciousness of Christ*, William Most, Christendom College Press, 1980, pp. 175-224.) Very similar was the work of Martin Dibelius, *The History of the Synoptic Tradition*, 1921.

Essenes A Jewish sect which practiced much asceticism and thought the worship in Jerusalem was not pure enough. They seem to be the same as those who lived chiefly at Qumran, on the western shore of the Dead Sea, from the second century B.C. to the second century A.D. Scrolls in jars in caves were found from this community beginning in 1947. At first some thought this discovery would undermine Christianity by showing the same doctrines were held there before Christ. This view is now abandoned. The writings are however useful in the study of Scripture.

Exegesis The work of determining the meaning of the texts of Scripture. Work begins with human techniques. For a Catholic, the final results must be checked by the Magisterium of the Church, which alone has the final right to determine the meaning of Scripture (Vatican II, *Constitution on Divine Revelation*, n. 10).

Existentialism A philosophy or group of philosophies which holds, falsely, that there are no general natures or truths (for example, I can say God made me, but cannot say He made all things) and so no general moral principles (cannot say adultery in general is right or wrong). Its influence is still strong, though somewhat on the wane. Logically, there is no room for a God in such a philosophy, since in it the universe does not make sense. There is no order in the universe; everything just "happens." Yet some existentialists claim to believe in God. The opposite is essentialism.

Evolution The theory that the human body developed from primates. See pp. 62-65 and also added comments below under polygenism.

Form criticism A method of Scripture study first developed by Hermann Gunkel (1862-1932) for the Old Testament, then applied to the New Testament by Rudolf Bultmann (1919) and Martin Dibelius (1921), and their followers. Though now much modified the basic ideas are still prominent today. In form criticism it is held, for example, that the Gospels originated in three stages: (1) The words and acts of Jesus. He would adapt His words to the audience on hand. (2) The way the Apostles and others in the first generation reported what He did and said. Again, with adaptation in wording or presentation to the current audience. (3) Some individuals in the Church, the Evangelists, under inspiration, wrote down some part of this basic preaching from stage 2. Thus the Gospels were born. This view is surely true thus far. The critics then seek to determine at which stage a passage of the Gospel took its present form, in the hope of finding more light. Difficulties arise because it is difficult to prove where the divisions come, and because so many form critics disbelieve in the supernatural, in miracles or real prophecies. Rather they believe that the first community was creative, that is, would make up things irresponsibly. The Pontifical Biblical Commission in 1964 (see chapter 20) said the method may be used, but with much care because of the prejudices, and the lack of firm proof. The study of the first two

184

stages just mentioned is, strictly, form criticism; the study of the changes made in stage 3 is redaction criticism.

Genre A pattern of writing with its own rules of how to write it and how to understand it. see pp. 49-51

Gnosticism A movement outside of Christianity (and so not strictly a heresy) beginning in the first century A.D. Gnostics place great stress on knowledge (gnosis) as the means of salvation. There are many varieties, and some of this kind of thought was even found at Qumran. The fully gnostic systems had in common two starting points: the majesty of God, and a belief that a series of aeons were between Him and the world. The aeons were in male-female pairs. God produced the first pair; that pair produced the next, and so on. They gradually became less perfect, and finally evil. Evil aeons produced our world. A whole library of original gnostic documents was found at Chenoboskion (nag-Hammadi) in Egypt in 1946. Some today claim, very foolishly, that what is now orthodoxy was merely the faction that finally won out. At first Gnosticism was on an equal footing. But we can see instances in the New Testament, especially in Paul's Epistle to the Colossians (and perhaps Ephesians) that the writer uses gnostic terms precisely to combat Gnosticism. Paul may, instead, be fighting Jewish apocalyptic speculations.

Hyksos These were foreign invaders who ruled Egypt (c. 1684-1567 A.D.) just before the New Kingdom period. Some think Joseph entered Egypt during this period, and that his good acceptance was due in part to the fact that some of the Hyksos were Semites. But if we accept the historicity of the Joseph narrative in Genesis, the reason was rather his successful interpretation, by God's help, of the dreams of the Pharaoh.

Inerrancy The doctrine that the Scriptures, when properly understood (using genre approach, etc.), are free of any kind of error.

Inspiration The doctrine that the chief author of Scripture is the Holy Spirit, who, being transcendent (beyond all our categories), can and does use a human writer as a secondary author in such a way that the human writes what the Holy Spirit wishes, without error, though the human retains his own style, perhaps even to the point of using some poor grammar.

Limbo The word refers to the state which most theologians think is that of infants who die without baptism—a state of natural happiness, but without the vision of God. The Church has not pronounced on this theory. There is also a Limbo of the Patriarchs, the state in which the just of the Old Testament period stayed until Christ had died, even though they had been sufficiently purified otherwise for the vision of God.

Literary patterns Same as genre above.

Midrash Some authors think it is a rather free literary genre with a core of history, but with additions and developments made in a meditative way, especially with the help of the Old Testament (see A. Wright, *The Literary Genre Midrash*, Alba House, Staten Island, 1967). Others, more rightly, think it merely means a particular ancient Jewish way of interpreting Scripture, in which one thing is read in terms of some other. (See Jacob Neusner, *Midrash in Context*, Fortress: Philadelphia, 1983.)

Mishnah The first great Jewish basic document produced after the fall of Jerusalem (70 A.D.). It dates from around 200 A.D. and set an authoritative pattern for later Judaism. The great Babylonian Talmud (completed 500-600 A.D.) quotes extensively from Mishnah with comments and additions.

Multiple fulfillment The view that scriptural prophecies, being divine, can be fulfilled more than once (see chapter 5).

Myth Scripture scholars do not mean by myth a mere fairy tale, but an ancient story, designed to convey certain things that really happened (see pp. 64-65).

Pentateuch The first five books of the Old Testament: Genesis, Exodus, Leviticus, Numbers, Deuteronomy.

Polygenism The theory that the human race descended from more than one pair (see p. 64). We can add that many more scholars today are now accepting basically the views of Allan Wilson (see *Newsweek*, January 11, 1988, pp. 46-52).

Qumran A site near the west shore of the Dead Sea where a very strict Jewish sect lived, who most probably were the Essenes (see Essenes above). Beginning in 1947, important scrolls have been found there, some of which are copies of parts of the Old Testament (earlier than our oldest manuscripts); others are documents of the community.

Rationalism The theory that reason, and not the acceptance of any teaching authority or revelation, is the only valid basis for belief or action.

Redaction The work of the human author in editing the tradition that he had at hand. This refers to the third stage mentioned above in the entry on form criticism.

Revelation God's self-communication to the human race. It involves giving new information, and thus differs from inspiration, which in itself does not give new information but only guidance and protection in setting things down. Vatican Council II (*Constitution on Divine Revelation*, n. 4) teaches that public revelation (that found in Scripture and Tradition, which was complete with the death of the last Apostle and the completion of the New Testament) is finished. There is to be no more revelation until the glorious return of Christ at the end. This is in contrast to all other revelations which are termed private, even if, like Fatima, they are addressed to the whole world. Some catechists today focus exclusively, or almost so, on revelation in a loose sense and interior guidance given to each individual today, to the practical exclusion of public revelation as interpreted by the Church.

Sheol The abode of the dead, as Jews conceived it during Old Testament times.

Structuralism (Semiotic analysis) An approach to Scripture study which holds there are three types or levels of structure: (1) the surface structures, those of "enunciation" limited in expression by the author, individuals or groups and their situations in life; (2) cultural structures, bounded by the "constraints" (limitations) proper to the culture in which the author lives; (3) the deep structures, those that are common to man as man. Structuralists focus on this third level (see chapter 24).

Synoptics The first three Gospels: Matthew, Mark, Luke.

Targums Ancient Jewish documents which include a translation into Aramaic from Hebrew that is usually rather free, and which includes fill-ins that show how the texts were understood by ancient Jews. We have them for nearly all of the Old Testament, in some places four different Targums. Dates are much debated. However, added evidence can be derived from the great survey of Jewish interest in the Messiah from the Mishnah (c. 200 A.D.) to the Babylonian Talmud (finished 500-600 A.D.), made by the great Jewish scholar, Jacob Neusner, in his *Messiah in Context* (Fortress, Philadelphia, 1984). There was scant interest in the Mishnah up to the Talmud. Even then, the only point of the major Old Testament prophecies on the Messiah mentioned is that he is to come from the line of David. In contrast, the Targums see many Messianic prophecies, giving much more detail. Hence it seems most likely that the parts of the Targums giving these prophecies are earlier than the Mishnah. For certain, the Targums show how the Jews understood the Old Testament prophecies without the help of "hindsight," that is, seeing them fulfilled in Christ, whom they hated.

Textual criticism Studying the text of a document such as the New Testament to ascertain whether it has come down to us in at least basically the form in which it was first written. For some ancient works, such as Julius Caesar, the gap between the original (autograph) and our oldest manuscript is nearly 1,000 years. For the New Testament, it is far less, and we have added means of checking on the interval. Further, the variations in readings in all manuscripts of the New Testament are mostly rather small and do not affect any basic doctrines, especially not the things needed for apologetics, sketched in chapter 2.

Tradition The process in which the original oral teaching of the Church has been passed on to later generations, including our own. In a narrow sense, the word sometimes refers to that which is found in the works of the Fathers of the Church and official documents during the first age of the Church. Form criticism, with its explanation of the three stages in the development of the Gospels (see Form criticism above), has done a good service in showing that the Gospels are just part of the ongoing teaching, set down under inspiration. Hence, in this sense Scripture and Tradition are one, or come from one source. Of course, we gain some truths from this oral transmission that are not found in writing in Scripture.

Ugarit An ancient city on the site of modern Ras Shamra, eight miles north of Latakia. It was on the coast of Syria and an important trading city. Its ruins were first found by chance in 1928. Many excavations have taken place since that time. Much ancient literature has been found there in Ugaritic, a Semitic language related to Hebrew. Both the literature and the language have been helpful in the study of the Old Testament.

Vulgate The Latin translation of the entire Bible made by St. Jerome. It stems from the request given St. Jerome by Pope Damasus in 364 that he revise the Old Latin translations of the Gospels. Jerome went further. He translated the entire Bible from the original languages. (He may have merely revised the translations of the Gospels.) Since his work was not well accepted at first, the old versions remained side by side with his for a long period, resulting in mixtures of the texts. The Council of Trent in 1546 called for a better edition of the Vulgate, but little was accomplished. A commission was appointed by St. Pius X in 1907 to really work on the text. The new text was promulgated by Pope John Paul II in 1979. The quality of St. Jerome's work is variable, but in general rather good. The Council of Trent declared his text "authentic," that is, valid for argumentation from Scripture. This statement was misunderstood and taken to mean that translations could be made only from the Vulgate. Pius XII, in 1943, in *Divino Afflante Spiritu*, corrected the error. He encouraged translations also from the original languages. (Vulgate stands for *Vulgata versio*, common version.)

INDEX